beautifully bold
faux flowers

Sylvia Hague

A QUANTUM BOOK

First edition for the United States, its territories and
possessions, Canada, and the Philippines published
in 2013 by Barron's Educational Series, Inc.

All inquiries should be addressed to:

Barron's Educational Series, Inc.
250 Wireless Boulevard
Hauppauge, New York 11788
www.barronseduc.com
ISBN: 978-1-4380-0173-9
Library of Congress Control Number: 2012949150

This book is published and produced by
Quantum Books
6 Blundell Street
London N7 9BH

QUMBBFF

Printed and bound in China

Publisher: Sarah Bloxham
Managing Editor: Samantha Warrington
Writer: Caroline Smith
Assistant Editor: Jo Morley
Design: Dave Jones
Photographer: Simon Pask and Elizabeth Zeschin
Production Manager: Rohana Yusof

All images are the copyright of Quantum Publishing

beautifully bold
faux flowers

Sylvia Hague

BARRON'S

CONTENTS

INTRODUCTION

The variety of faux flowers never ceases to amaze me! I've been lucky enough to have been working with these beautiful blooms for many years, and I still get immense pleasure creating new arrangements. The detail and refinement of silk flowers is such that even I find it hard to tell them from the real thing! And the range of blooms now available has meant I've been able to specialize in creating designs that delight and uplift, and which are very personal to my clients.

In this book, I've put together 25 displays that I hope really have the "wow" factor. In the first chapter, you'll find some truly grand and gorgeous displays that are sure to impress on sheer size alone. In chapter 2, I've put together a set of striking arrangements using simple, elegant design principles. For the third chapter, I've gone with some bright, bold color choices to create stunning, vivid displays.

The range of faux flowers is incredible; there's a color and shape for almost every purpose. If you look at the Faux Flower Spectrum here, or go to www.silkflowersbysylvia.com, you'll see the wealth of blooms available. For the arrangements featured in this book, I've picked those flowers that seem most bold and beautiful to me. However, tastes differ and your favorites may not be the same as mine. But whatever flowers you choose to use, you can still follow the techniques and design advice included in this book to create your own individual arrangements.

I hope this book encourages you to explore the bold and beautiful world of faux flowers, and I hope that they give you as much pleasure as they have given me.

Sylvia Hague

Sylvia Hague

GALLERY OF ARRANGEMENTS

In this book, you will find 25 gorgeous silk flower arrangements. There are big, bold displays and simple yet stunning arrangements, as well as exciting ideas for combining colors. On these pages you will find snapshots of each beautiful display.

Part of the appeal of faux flowers lies in the great variety of different blooms and foliage available – just as in nature, there are flowers to suit every taste and to fit every situation. No matter what style your decor is, or your personal preference, you will find there is a wide range of faux flowers from which you can create the perfect display.

If you want an arrangement for a larger reception room or entrance hall, then it's the ideal opportunity to use some of the larger faux flowers. Tall stems and large flower heads will ensure maximum impact – blooms such as the giant alliums used in "Sensational Centerpiece" (see page 14), or the extra-tall white orchids of "Thoroughly Modern" (see page 28). Dramatic and unusual flowers, such as the slipper orchids in "Rare and Refined" (see page 23), will always attract the eye and create a real focal point in any room. And arrangements don't have to be huge in order to attract attention – a simple combination of strong shapes and pure colors can be just as effective. The teaming of a plain cylindrical vase with bold, round, white and magenta peonies in "Fun and Fabulous" (see page 46) is a perfect example.

Being creative with color is another way in which you can make the most of faux flowers. You can take a subtle approach and pick blooms in a gentle shade – as in "Beautiful Blues" (see page 64) – or go for real show-stopping colors – such as in "Strike a Pose" (see page 67). Whatever your style, this book is bound to inspire your own faux flower designs.

SENSATIONAL CENTERPIECE *pages 14–16*

MAKING AN ENTRANCE *pages 17–19*

MAGNIFICENT MAGNOLIAS *pages 20–22*

RARE AND REFINED *pages 23–24*

ABSOLUTELY ELEGANT *pages 25–27*

THOROUGHLY MODERN *pages 28–29*

STYLISH IN SILVER *pages 30–31*

EXOTIC OVERTURE *pages 32–33*

OPULENT ORCHIDS *pages 34–35*

THE PERFECT PAIR *pages 38–39*

PURE AND BRIGHT *pages 40–41*

ALL-AROUND PERFORMANCE *pages 42–43*   THE ULTIMATE CHIC *pages 44–45*   FUN AND FABULOUS *pages 46–48*

GRACE AND SPLENDOR *pages 49–51*   SIMPLY SUBLIME *pages 52–53*

LIGHT AND LOVELY *pages 54–55*

GLORIOUS COLOR *pages 58–59*

GRAND GESTURE *pages 60–61*

PRETTY IN PINK *pages 62–63*

BEAUTIFUL BLUES *pages 64–66*

STRIKE A POSE *pages 67–68*

BOLD STATEMENT *pages 69–71*

SHOCKING PINK *pages 72–73*

COUNTRY CHARM *pages 74–75*

CHAPTER 1

Big and Bold

When you want a faux flower arrangement that makes a real impression, there's nothing quite like choosing big, bold statement blooms to create something truly grand and gorgeous. And the beauty of these displays is that you can enjoy their glory for years to come.

SENSATIONAL CENTERPIECE

Nothing makes a real impression like a stunning centerpiece, and the giant flower heads of these purple alliums surely have the wow factor. Sharp spikes of meadow grass are a perfect foil for the frothy, round allium flowers.

You will need

- Cylindrical glass vase, about 20 in (50 cm) tall and 8 in (20 cm) in diameter
- Small glass vase
- 4 tied clumps of meadow grass
- 7 large purple alliums
- 5 onion grass

1 Place two of the clumps of meadow grass in the larger glass vase. Then put the smaller vase inside, placing it in the middle of the larger vase. Your smaller vase can be anything – a jelly jar would do or a carafe as shown here – but it needs to be small enough so that you can fit the grass in around the outside.

2 Slip the remaining clumps of grass into the vase, between the smaller vase and the outside of the larger vase. If necessary, tease the grass leaves apart a bit to help obscure the small inner vase.

3 Take one allium and place it in the inner vase; let the flower fall forward very slightly. Take a second allium and place it behind the first and just to the right; let this one fall slightly to the right. Take another flower and place it just behind the first allium. The flower heads should stand about 4 in (10 cm) taller than the tops of the grass, with the last allium added being slightly taller than the others.

Design ideas

This display is all about structure, and the large flower heads are what give the arrangement its focal point. If you want something different, then try white alliums instead of the purple. This will work particularly well if you are placing the vase against a dark background.

4 ————————————————

Take the remaining alliums and trim a small amount off the stems so they are 1¼–1½ in (3–4 cm) shorter than the three in the vase. Take one allium and bend the stem slightly into a curve. Push the stem into the inner vase through the front two grass clumps, so that the flower head leans outward and slightly to the right, toward the front of the display.

5 ————————————————

Bend the stem of another allium and push it in the inner vase in roughly the same place as the last flower. Let this lean out toward the left. Bend the stem of another flower and push this in at the back left; let this lean out to the left. Bend the stem of the last flower a bit more than the others and push it in at the left-hand side, between the grass clumps but not into the inner vase.

6 ————————————————

Take the stems of onion grass and slip them into the back of the display, fanning them out slightly behind the flower heads. The twining shapes they make should fill the white space between the allium flowers. Step back and check the flower positions. Although this display is an asymmetric design, make sure the outward curving flowers do not lean out too far.

MAKING AN ENTRANCE

For a truly theatrical display, these striking moth orchids are real showstoppers. Their unusual flowers, combined with their tall stems, are ideal if you want to create a dramatic arrangement that adds a touch of class to any setting.

You will need

- Plain, square-topped container, about 12 in (30 cm) wide and 12 in (30 cm) deep
- Oasis foam
- Oasis adhesive
- Moss
- Bent wire pins (optional)
- 7 clumps of moth-orchid leaves
- 7 pale lime-green moth orchids
- 2 twisted twigs
- 10–12 plant stakes
- Raffia or floral wire

1 Fill your chosen container with Oasis foam. Secure it in place using the adhesive. Then arrange some moss over the top of the Oasis, so that all the foam is concealed. Insert bent wire pins to hold the moss in place. Alternatively, secure the moss with a few dots of Oasis adhesive. Insert two clumps of moth-orchid leaves at the center.

2 Take two more clumps of foliage and push these into the Oasis to the left of the central clumps. Make sure you have one clump toward the front of the container and one toward the back. Arrange the attached aerial roots so that they fall over the edge of the container.

3 Take two more leaf clumps and push these into the Oasis to the right of center, with one toward the back and one toward the front. Push the remaining clump into the center front. Take one moth orchid and push the stem into the center of the display. Push it down so that the flower stands about 8 in (20 cm) above the leaves.

4 Take one twisted twig and push it into the center, close to the flower stem. Add a plant stake at roughly the same position. Push another support into the Oasis slightly to the left of the first.

Design ideas

This display uses wooden plant stakes as an important design feature. They do have a function – some are used to help support the orchid stems – but there are more plant supports used than there are flowers. The strong vertical lines of the stakes contrast with the soft lines of the flowers and foliage.

Sylvia says...

I love the unusual color of these moth orchids. The pale lime-green flowers are tinged with a darker green at the center and then veined with a dark burgundy color. If you look at each bloom carefully, the contrast between the green and the burgundy is quite striking. Despite this, the overall effect is subtle, and these orchids have a cool and distinctive grandeur, making them ideal blooms for a dramatic display.

5

Push another orchid into the Oasis, next to the last stake you inserted. Push the stem in so the flowerhead is roughly level with the first bloom. Add another orchid, pushing it in close to the central support. Don't push this one in so far; it should stand taller than the other two. Use floral wire to tie the flower stems to their adjacent supports. Add two more supports to the right of center.

6

Add another moth orchid to the right of center. Arrange it so the flower leans out toward the front left. Add another that leans out toward the front right. Secure the stems to the adjacent stake. Push the remaining twisted twig in at the center.

7

Add some more stakes; you should have used a total of ten to twelve stakes. Space them evenly across the width of the display. Take the remaining two moth orchids and push them into the front of the display. Arrange them so that they fall further forward than the other flowers, and push the stems in a bit further so that these flower heads are at a lower level.

MAGNIFICENT MAGNOLIAS

At the heart of this grand display is the pure white simplicity of magnolia flowers. Their timeless beauty makes them the perfect choice when you are looking for the ideal blooms for a classic and stylish arrangement.

You will need

- Shallow ceramic dish, about 14 in (35 cm) in diameter
- Oasis foam
- Oasis adhesive
- Moss
- Bent wire pins (optional)
- 9 stems of magnolia
- 9–10 sprigs of magnolia foliage
- 3 stems of twisted pussy willow

1 ———————————

Fill your chosen dish with Oasis foam. Secure it with Oasis adhesive. Arrange some moss over the top of the Oasis so that the foam, particularly at the edges, is concealed. Use adhesive or bent wire pins to secure the moss in place.

2 ———————————

Take one magnolia stem and push it into the Oasis foam at the very center of the dish. This stem is going to set the highest point in the display, so don't push it in too far. Put a small amount of adhesive on the end of the stem before pushing it into the foam to secure it.

Design ideas

The container used for this arrangement is decorated with a simple Chinese-style design. The Oriental imagery works well with the look of the magnolias. If you don't have a similarly decorated dish, you could use a plain, single-colored ceramic bowl: just make sure that it is a low, shallow shape.

3 ———————————

Take another magnolia stem and place it slightly in front of the first one; this should be at roughly the same height as the first stem. Take another magnolia and push it in at the right, so it leans out toward the right at a lower level. Similarly, add another magnolia stem at the left of the display.

4 ———————————

Take three shorter stems – you may have to trim the stem length slightly – and push these into the Oasis at the front of the dish, with one at the center and one on either side of this. Angle the stems so they lean outward.

5

Take the remaining two magnolia stems and insert these on either side of the existing flowers in the dish. Step back and look at the display to make sure that you have a balanced arrangement of flowers, with the tallest stems at the center and the shortest at the front.

6

Take two sprigs of foliage and insert on either side of the display so that they lean outward over the edge of the dish. Take two more sprigs and insert them at the back so they fan up behind the magnolia stems.

Design ideas

Although this display is basically symmetrical, the branching shapes of the magnolia stems break up the arrangement, giving it an open, natural look. Twisted pussy willow stems, with their small, frothy flower heads, add to this effect.

7

Take some more foliage sprigs – you should need about five or six – and insert these all around the base of the arrangement so they fill the space between the bottom flowers and the top of the moss-covered Oasis. Let the leaves fall forward and over the edge of the dish.

8

Take one of the twisted pussy willow stems and push it into the very center of the display so it weaves in among the magnolia. Add another twisted pussy willow to the right, and one to the left.

RARE AND REFINED

These exotic and unusual orchids are just what's needed when you want to make a real statement.
All they need as partners are some spikey grass leaves and a plain, unadorned
metallic vase – a study in simplicity.

You will need

- Cylindrical metal or metal-like vase, about 16 in (40 cm) tall and 5 in (12 cm) diameter
- 1 tied clump of meadow grass
- All-purpose adhesive (optional)
- 5 tall lady slipper orchids

1

Take the clump of meadow grass and place it in the vase. If you wish, you can secure it in a central position in the vase by squeezing some small drops of adhesive onto the base of the grass clump and then pressing the grass into the vase.

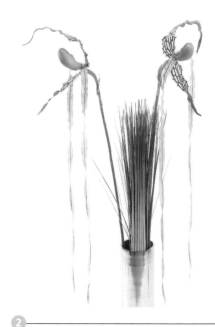

2

Take two of the lady slipper orchids and place them in the vase, toward the back of the grass clump. Again, if you wish to secure them in the vase, place a small drop of adhesive on the end of each stem before putting the flowers in the vase.

Sylvia says...

These lady slipper orchids are among the more unusual orchids available in silk. At the center of each bloom is a pouch: in nature, this serves to trap the insects that pollinate the plant; in faux flowers, the feature is an eye-catching focal point. Above and below the pouch are strongly marked, ruffled petals – both a pale lemon, blotched with dark, red-brown lines. On either side of the pouch are extended petals, each one almost as long as the flower's stem itself. These are marked in a similar way to the upper and lower petals, but in subtler shades. These unusual floral features combine to give you an exotic-looking faux flower that's ideal for striking displays.

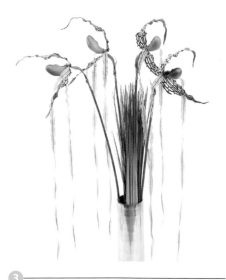

3

Place two more lady slipper orchids in the front of the vase, and to either side of the meadow grass clump. Arrange these two flowers so they lean outward and to either side. Secure with adhesive as before, if desired.

4

Take the remaining lady slipper orchid and push it into the vase at the very front center. Let this bloom lean forwards. Make sure the long, extended petals of each flower are not tangled and that they fall downward evenly.

ABSOLUTELY ELEGANT

The serene beauty of these cymbidium orchids makes the perfect focal point in any room. Each flower bears slender petals, lightly dusted with a speckling of dark pink, set around a golden-yellow center. The slim upright leaves give the display a strong structure.

You will need

- Cube-shaped ceramic container, about 10 in (25 cm) square
- Oasis foam
- Oasis adhesive
- Moss
- Bent wire pins (optional)
- 7 cymbidium orchid clumps, with foliage attached
- 4 onion grass stems

1

Fill your chosen container with Oasis foam and secure it in place with adhesive. Scatter some moss over the top of the Oasis to conceal the foam. Use some drops of adhesive or some bent wire pins to hold the moss in place if desired.

2

Take two of the cymbidium clumps and insert into the Oasis foam toward the back of container. Position so they are centered along the back edge of the container. Dab the ends of the clumps with a little adhesive before pushing into the foam to help secure more effectively.

3

Take one onion grass stem and push it into the foam just to the right of the right-hand orchid. Don't push it in too far; make this the tallest element in the display. Take another onion grass stem and push this into the foam to the left of the left-hand orchid. Then take the remaining onion grass and push one in just in front of the right-hand orchid and one just in front of the left-hand orchid.

Sylvia says...

"I've used one of my favorite containers for this display. The traditional decoration of flowers and insects strikes me as being ideal for a classic orchid arrangement like this one. Because I use it over and over again for different faux flower arrangements, I don't mind that the Oasis foam is glued into the container. I have to refresh the foam occasionally, but otherwise I simply reuse the container with a change of plants. If you have a favorite container and you want to be able to use it for other purposes – for fresh flowers say, or for a potted plant – then find a cheap plastic pot that fits very snugly inside your vase. Glue the Oasis into the plastic pot and then slip that into your container. The plastic pot needs to fit tightly in your vase to prevent the display from toppling over."

4 Take another cymbidium clump and push this into the display in front of the existing flowers and centered between them. Use some adhesive on the end of the stem to help secure the clump. Bend the stem so that the flower head falls outward and forward over the edge of the container.

5 Take another orchid clump and push it in on the right and toward the back of the container; add another to the left and toward the back. Bend the stems slightly so that the flower heads lean outward. Do the same with the leaves so that they extend beyond the edge of the container.

6 Take the last two cymbidium clumps and push one into the foam at the front right, and one in at the front left. Push them a little further into the foam so the flower heads sit slightly lower than the last two inserted. Bend the stems on these two flowers so that they lean outward and toward the front of the display. Bend the leaves into curves that echo the curves of the flower stems.

THOROUGHLY MODERN

For an up-to-date arrangement to suit any setting – traditional or contemporary – these cool, classic white moth orchids are just the answer. The unusual test-tube-like container makes the most of the long, slender stems of these flowers and the accompanying allium buds.

You will need

- Test-tube-style container with 6 individual tubes of varying lengths—the tallest about 3 ft (1 m) in length—set in a rectangular base
- White decorative pebbles
- 6 large white moth orchids
- 6 allium buds

1 Fill the test tubes with pebbles to a depth of 6–10 in (15–25 cm). Don't drop them in—they might break the ends of the tubes. Instead, hold the tubes horizontally and insert the pebbles. Then gradually tilt the tubes until the pebbles slide to the end. Take two moth orchids and put them in the two tallest tubes, toward the back of the base. Push the stems gently between the pebbles.

2 Place two more moth orchids into the middle-sized tubes, at the left and right of the display. Push their stems in between the pebbles. Bend the flower stems so that the blooms lean forward and out to the left and right of the display.

3 Take the remaining two orchids and put these in the shortest tubes, at the front of the base, pushing the stems in between the pebbles. Bend the stems of these two orchids a bit more than the previous two, so that the flower heads fall forward and to the front at a lower level. You may need to trim a couple of inches off their stems.

4 Then take the allium buds and put one in each test tube, making sure the ends of their stems are concealed by either the pebbles or the orchid stems. Bend the stems of the allium buds so they lean out toward the fronts and sides, and so that the shape they make complements the shape of the orchids.

Sylvia says...

When I found the unusual container that I've used for this display, I was sure it would be ideal for something – but I just wasn't sure what at first! Then one day, I was creating a display using large moth orchids with incredibly long stems. I was just trimming the ends off the stems to fit a vase when it struck me – these would be ideal for the test-tube-style container sitting in my store room. A few white pebbles at the bottom of each glass tube were all that was needed to hold the extra-long stems in place. But I felt that the display still needed an extra element. There was no foliage that suited the container, but I did have some buds of giant alliums. Their stems were long enough to combine with the orchids, and their slender linear form complemented the flowers' shape perfectly.

STYLISH IN SILVER

The frothy flower heads of Queen Anne's Lace are combined with stems of furry pussy willow in this simple, silvery display. A contrast in textures is created by mixing the soft shapes of the flowers with the harder lines of meadow grass, and setting it all in an angular-shaped vase.

You will need

- Rectangular metallic vase, about 16 in (40 cm) tall and 5 in (12 cm) wide
- 12 stems of pussy willow
- 3 clumps of meadow grass
- 12–15 individual leaves of meadow grass
- 6 Queen Anne's Lace

1 Set the vase down with a corner facing toward you. Place one pussy willow stem in the vase so that it leans into the back corner. Add two more pussy willows so that these stems lean into the outer corners of the vase. Add a pussy willow stem between the back stem and the left-hand stem, and one between the back stem and the right-hand stem. Make these lean backward.

2 Take the remaining pussy willow stems and arrange them in front of the first stems. Use the stems of the pussy willow already in the vase as supports for the new additions. Make sure that the pussy willow fans out evenly across the width of the display.

Design ideas

There is no supporting medium used in this display. Instead, the shape of the vase is exploited to hold the flowers in place. The container has a square opening and is used with a corner facing forward, rather than a flat side. The flower stems fall sideways, backward and forward and are supported in the corners of the vase.

3 Take the clumps of meadow grass and put one in the center of the display, with the remaining two on either side. If necessary, tease out the grass leaves so that they fan out in front of the pussy willow stems.

4 Take the Queen Anne's Lace and add this to the vase so that it stands in front of the pussy willow. Arrange the flowers so that they are spaced evenly in a fan shape. Take the separate grass leaves and insert them throughout the display; don't push them in too deep, as you want the spikes to stand slightly above the other flowers.

EXOTIC OVERTURE

These fabulous orchids bear truly striking blooms. Small, star-like individual flowers emerge from between three larger, strongly marked petals – each one veined with burgundy and streaked with blush pink. The pale-lemon and lime-green coloring of these orchids is particularly vivid.

You will need

- Tall, slightly ovoid glass vase, about 20 in (50 cm) tall and 6–7 in (15–18 cm) in diameter
- Lime-green decorative sand
- 6 large green taca orchids

1 Tip some lime-green decorative sand into the vase to a depth of 3¼–4 in (8–10 cm). Do this gently to avoid scratching the surface of the glass. Then tip the vase so the top of the sand is sloped at an angle. Set the vase in front of you so the lower side of the sloping sand faces you.

2 Take one orchid and place it in the vase, pushing the stem into the center of the sand and angling the stem so the flower leans to the left. Add another orchid with the stem pushed in the sand a bit behind the first one; this flower should also lean toward the left.

3 Add another orchid so the stem is close to the others and the flower head falls forward over the edge of the vase at the front. Take another orchid and place it in the vase so the flower head is just to the right of the last one you added.

4 Place another orchid in the vase so the flower on this one is to the right of the display. Add another just to the right and a little behind the last. All the flower heads should be roughly level and facing outward from the center.

Design ideas

The support for these tall-stemmed flowers is simply some decorative sand, available from floral suppliers. A small amount, poured into the bottom of the vase, is enough to hold the stems in place. Tilting the vase to one side will alter the level of the sand and create additional visual interest.

OPULENT ORCHIDS

If you want to make a grand gesture, then it's worth pulling out all the stops! Choose big, bold blooms and a strongly shaped container. A classic urn, with its architectural style, is combined with magnificent moth orchids for a glorious and gorgeous display.

You will need

- Large urn-like container, about 18 in (45 cm) tall and about 12 in (30 cm) in diameter
- Oasis foam
- Oasis adhesive
- Moss
- Bent wire pins (optional)
- 5 clumps of moth orchid leaves
- 9 moth orchids
- 9 plant stakes
- Raffia or floral wire

1 ————————————————

Fill your urn with Oasis foam and secure it in place with the adhesive. Arrange some moss over the top of the foam so that the Oasis is concealed, particularly around the edge. Secure with glue or bent wire pins if desired. Push one clump of leaves in at the center. Then push two more in toward the front, and two more in toward the back.

2 ————————————————

Take two of the moth orchids and push them into the Oasis toward the back of the container and a little way apart. Don't push in too far; these are the highest point in the display. Insert plant stakes next to each flower and use raffia or wire to tie the stems to the stakes. Bend the stems slightly so the flower heads lean to the left and right.

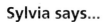

3 ————————————————

Add two more orchids to the front of the display, spacing them a little closer together than the first two flowers. Push them in a little deeper so they are slightly lower than the first two. Insert stakes next to these orchids and secure the stems to the supports with raffia or floral wire.

4 ————————————————

Take the remaining five orchids and push them into the foam all around the container, outside the central four orchids. Push these in a bit deeper than the others so that the flower heads are at a lower level. Make sure the blooms fall forward and outward. Add plant stakes close to each orchid and secure with raffia or wire ties.

CHAPTER 2

Keep it Simple

Less is more, as they say, and this is quite true when it comes to designing your faux flower displays. With a limited palette of colors or a minimal selection of only one, or maybe two, flower types, you can create an arrangement that's simple yet stunning to look at.

THE PERFECT PAIR

When you want to brighten up a stylish but neutral contemporary interior, there is nothing like bright pink flowers. Temper the effect by pairing a pot of magenta orchids with a matching container of more subtly shaded blooms.

You will need

- 2 matching ceramic pots, each 8 in (20 cm) tall and 6 in (15 cm) in diameter
- Oasis foam
- Oasis adhesive
- Moss
- Bent wire pins (optional)
- 2 clumps of moth orchid leaves
- 2 small magenta moth orchids
- 2 small pale-colored moth orchids
- 4 plant stakes
- Raffia or floral wire

1 —————————

Fill the first pot with Oasis foam. Secure it in place using the adhesive, then arrange some moss over the top of the Oasis to conceal the foam. Use bent wire pins or some adhesive to hold the moss in place, if desired. Insert one clump of moth orchid leaves at the center. Repeat to fill the second pot with foam and add the leaves.

2 —————————

Take one of the magenta orchids and push it into the foam at the center of the first pot, close to the leaves. Angle the stem so it leans very slightly to the left. Take one of the pale-colored orchids and insert it in the second pot, in a position that matches the magenta orchid in the first pot.

Design ideas

You can create quite a different style of display using the same orchids and container – all you need to do is subtly alter the way the flowers are arranged. Trim the length of the stems so they are much shorter and then bend the flower heads into a more exaggerated curve to create a more compact design.

3 —————————

Take the remaining magenta orchid and push it into the center of the first pot, just to the right of the first flower. Let this one lean to the right slightly. Repeat with the remaining pale-colored orchid and the second pot.

4 —————————

Take two of the plant stakes and insert them in the first pot, close to the orchid stems; angle the stakes so they lean slightly out to the left and to the right. Secure the stems to the stakes with raffia or wire. Add the remaining plant stakes to the second pot.

PURE AND BRIGHT

A big basket of beautiful, pure white hydrangeas will brighten up any corner of your home. The large, spreading flower heads of these classic blooms are made up of a myriad of smaller flowers. Massed together in a single display, the effect is dramatic.

You will need

- Wide, circular basket, about 8 in (20 cm) deep and 18 in (45 cm) in diameter
- Oasis foam
- Oasis adhesive
- Moss
- Bent wire pins (optional)
- 10 white hydrangeas
- 8–10 hydrangea leaves

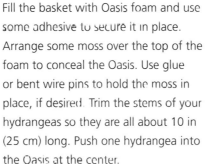

1 Fill the basket with Oasis foam and use some adhesive to secure it in place. Arrange some moss over the top of the foam to conceal the Oasis. Use glue or bent wire pins to hold the moss in place, if desired. Trim the stems of your hydrangeas so they are all about 10 in (25 cm) long. Push one hydrangea into the Oasis at the center.

2 Take three of the trimmed hydrangeas and push these into the Oasis foam around the first central flower. Keep the flowers fairly tightly packed together, but allow the tips of some of the attached leaves to peek through the petals.

3 Take the remaining hydrangeas and push them into the Oasis foam around the central clump of flowers. Angle the stems as you push them in so the flower heads face out and slightly upward. Space the flowers evenly apart. Take some extra hydrangea leaves and use these to fill in any gaps in between the flower heads. Tuck a few leaves in under the flowers, close to the edge of the basket and falling out over the edge.

ALL-AROUND PERFORMANCE

The ideal way to introduce a note of drama in an arrangment is to create an asymmetric design. Purple alliums lean to one side of this display, in a fan of perfect pompons, to be balanced by a twist of water lily stems inside the vase.

You will need

- Ovoid shallow glass vase, about 10 in (25 cm) tall and 3 in (7.5 cm) in diameter at the top
- 2 water lily leaves, with long attached stems
- 5 small purple alliums

1

Take one of the water lily leaves and curl the stem into a rough spiral shape. Put the stem in the vase so the leaf is at the top left side, and let the stem uncurl against the sides of the vase. Repeat with the other water lily leaf so the leaf sits on the top right side of the vase. Twist this leaf around so it's in a more upright position than the other.

2

Slip one of the alliums into the container at an angle from the right-hand side. The flower should extend out toward the right and lean at a pronounced angle. It should be resting on the right-hand upright water lily leaf. The end of the stem inside the vase should be up against the left-hand side of the vase.

Design ideas

3

Take another allium and slip it into the vase so its flower head rests on the first allium's flower head. Add another flower, resting its flower head on the second allium's flower head. Repeat to add another allium. The ends of the stems of the flowers should be pressed against the left-hand side of the vase.

4

Take the last allium and slip it into the vase so that its flower head is level with but in front of the four alliums already in the vase. The stem should rest more on the front of the right-hand water lily leaf. The end of this stem should be pressed against the back of the vase.

Allium flowers come in white and purple, and there are two shades of purple available – a light purple and a darker violet shade. This display uses both purple shades, but you could confine your selection to just one. Or, try something different and choose white alliums.

THE ULTIMATE CHIC

For an ultra-modern, uber-fashionable minimalist decor you want a simple, pared-down faux flower display. These pure white amaryllis are the perfect blooms: hand-tied and set in a pebble-filled glass vase, this arrangement is simple yet chic.

You will need

- Cylindrical glass vase, about 12 in (30 cm) tall and 3¼ in (8 cm) in diameter
- 6 white amaryllis
- Raffia or floral wire
- White decorative pebbles

1

Gather the amaryllis into a bunch, arranging them carefully so that the blooms aren't too squashed together and so that they face upward and outward. When you are happy with the arrangement, use raffia or floral wire to bind the stems together. Wrap the raffia or wire around the stems close to the flower heads.

2

Fill the vase with white decorative pebbles to a depth of about 2 in (5 cm). Because the vase is glass, don't drop all the pebbles in at once; there is a chance this might break the bottom of the vase. Instead, take a small handful of pebbles and put your hand into the vase, to the bottom, and then release the pebbles. This also helps prevent the pebbles from scratching the sides of the vase.

3

Take the bunched amaryllis and put them in the vase. Push the stems into the center of the pebbles; you may have to use a slight twisting motion to work the ends of the stems in among the pebbles. Push the stems in to a depth of about 5/8 in (1.5 cm). Make sure the amaryllis bunch is standing upright and then slip some more pebbles into the vase, between the stems and the sides of the vase. Fill until the pebbles reach a depth of about 4 in (10 cm). Again, take care when adding the pebbles to avoid scratching or breaking the glass vase.

FUN AND FABULOUS

The key to this display's success is the use of contrast. Brilliant magenta peonies are contrasted with cool, creamy white ones, and the simple modern shape of the cylindrical glass vase is the ideal foil for these bold, blousy blooms.

You will need

- Shallow cylindrical glass vase, about 6 in (15 cm) tall and 10 in (25 cm) in diameter
- Oasis foam
- Oasis adhesive
- 3–4 aspidistra leaves
- Moss
- Bent wire pins (optional)
- 5 magenta peonies, stems trimmed to about 8 in (20 cm)
- 8 white peonies, stems trimmed to 8 in (20 cm) long
- 4–5 clumps of peony leaves

1 Cut the Oasis foam to fit your container, leaving a small gap between the foam and the sides of the vase. Glue it in place. Slip the aspidistra leaves in between the Oasis and the sides of the vase, making sure the leaves overlap and conceal the foam. Arrange moss over the top of the foam, securing it with adhesive or bent wire pins if desired.

2 Take one magenta peony and push the stem into the foam at an angle so the flower head points forward, slightly overlapping the edge of the vase. Take a white peony and push it into the foam to the right of the magenta peony; add one to the left. Angle the flowers so they point outward from the center and overlap the edge of the vase.

3 Take another magenta peony and push that into the foam next to one of the white peonies. Push another magenta peony in next to the other white peony. Now push in two more white peonies, next to the magenta ones you've just added. Finish with another magenta peony in the gap between the last two white flowers. You should have four white and four magenta peonies arranged in a ring around the edge of the vase, with all their flower heads pointing out from the center.

Sylvia says...

When you want to use a glass vase it can mean that you won't be able to use Oasis foam as a support for the flowers – useful as it is, the foam is not an attractive feature when seen through the sides of the vase! However, there is a useful trick you can employ to conceal the foam and still use the vase you want. Take some large faux leaves and use them to line the inside of the vase. Here, I've used aspidistra leaves – their length and width was ideal for this particular container – but there are others you can choose. Hydrangea leaves are quite large, as are anthurium leaves, but you can experiment with whatever you have. This trick is also a great way to use up any leftover foliage that you've trimmed off the stems of flowers.

4

Take the clumps of peony leaves and arrange them in a ring inside the first ring of peony flowers. Fan the leaves out – you may have to separate the clumps into individual leaves in order to arrange them correctly. The tips of the leaves should protrude slightly over the tops of the flowers.

5

Take a white peony and push it into the foam above the front-most magenta peony. Angle the stem so the flower points up and out from the center. Add three more white peonies, positioning them above the magenta peonies in the vase in the same way. Tweak the leaves so they are visible between the flowers.

6

Take the last magenta peony and insert it in the middle of the display, in the center of the ring of white peonies added at step 5. The stem should be upright so that the flower head points directly upward. The finished display should have a neat dome shape; you may have to push flowers further into the foam or pull them out slightly to adjust the arrangement as necessary.

GRACE AND SPLENDOR

Although this display uses just nine blooms and features only two different flower types, it has a distinct grandeur. Both the Casablanca lilies and hydrangeas used in this display have large, impressive flower heads that really make an impact.

You will need

- Globe-shaped glass vase, about 12 in (30 cm) in diameter
- 12–15 long individual grass leaves
- 5 large pale pink hydrangeas
- 4 large pale pink Casablanca lilies

1

Take the grass leaves and gather them up into a loose bunch. Wrap the bunch around your hand a few times and, holding on to the ends of the grass with your thumb, put your hand into the vase. Let go of the grass and the leaves should spring out to fill the vase. You want the leaves to form a random spiral shape, so you may have to adjust a few leaves to get a pleasing result.

2

Take one hydrangea and place it in the vase so the end of the stem is at the bottom of the vase and the flower head leans toward the right. Take a second hydrangea and place it in the vase so the stem balances on the stem of the first and the flower head leans to the left. The end of the stem can be touching the back of the vase.

3

Take one of the Casablanca lilies and place it in the center of the vase so the stem is upright and more or less vertical. The lily's stem can lean up against the hydrangea stems, nestling in the angle created by the crossing stems of the hydrangeas. Put the lily into the vase gently to avoid knocking the hydrangeas out of position.

Sylvia says...

There is no supporting medium used in this display – no Oasis foam, no acrylic water. Instead, the flower stems support each other. After putting the first flower in, you rest the second on the first and so on, until the arrangement is finished. I chose to build up the display in this way because I wanted to create somthing with a loose and naturalistic look – I wanted to keep the look of a great armful of flowers, freshly gathered from the garden. Of course a simple and natural look is often the hardest to achieve, and I had to take care with the placement of each flower. But the beauty of this display is that you can achieve a beautiful finished result without having to religiously copy the arrangement here. As long as you achieve a balance between the combined flowers, your display will be just as harmonious.

4

Take another hydrangea and insert it into the display from the back right Slide the stem between the existing stems in the vase so it is supported where the stems cross. Add another hydrangea at the back left, taking the same care when slipping it in among the existing flowers.

5

Now take another Casablanca lily and insert it into the display from the back left, between the two hydrangeas on the left. Angle the stem as you slip it in; the stem should be touching the right-hand side of the vase. Add another lily from the right-hand side, angling the stem so that the end touches the left-hand side of the vase at the top.

6

Take the remaining Casablanca lily and slip it into the display from the back between the two hydrangeas. Angle the stem so that its end is touching against the front side of the vase. Add the last hydrangea at the far right, inserting the stem so that it goes into the display almost sideways, with the end touching the left-hand side of the vase at the top. When you pick up the display to place it in your chosen setting, do so with care to avoid jostling the blooms and changing their position.

SIMPLY SUBLIME

This traditional display of stately classic tulips is given a twist with the addition of a latticework of delicate budding twigs. The criss-cross patterns created by the twigs break up the solid lines of the tulips' thick stems and fleshy leaves.

You will need

- Glass vase, about 12 in (30 cm) tall, 9 in (23 cm) in diameter
- 1 lattice of budding twigs
- 8 purple and green-tinged tulips

1 Fold in half the lattice of budding twigs and then slip it into the vase. Pull the twigs apart to open out the lattice a bit so the twigs spread across the width of the vase. Put your hand into the center, between the front and back of the lattice, and push it up against the front and back of the vase so you have room for the flowers.

2 Take the first tulip and put into the vase at the back left; add another at the back right. Make sure the flowers are inside the encircling lattice of twigs. Take the next two tulips and trim the stems slightly so they are a little shorter than the first tulips. Put these in the vase at front left and front right. Angle the flowers outward.

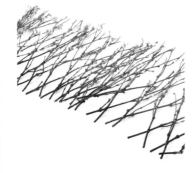

Design ideas

A lattice made up of connected budding twigs is used to line the glass vase before the tulips are added to the display. Because the fine twigs are interlocked to form one piece, there is no need to arrange lots of separate twigs, making this lattice an invaluable filler for faux-flower displays.

3 Take another two tulips and put these in the vase between the last two just added. Angle these so they face toward the front of the display, with one facing left and one facing just right of center. Adjust the petals so the blooms have a more open appearance.

4 Take the last remaining two tulips and put these in the center of the display, just behind the last two added. Allow these to point upward.

LIGHT AND LOVELY

Sometimes it's an understated display that make the greatest impact — the calm simplicity of these beautiful orchids adds a note of elegance to any room. The clean white flowers and glossy dark-green leaves can be combined harmoniously with any color and any style of decor.

You will need

- Plain, square-topped container, about 12 in (30 cm) wide and 10 in (5 cm) deep
- Oasis foam
- Oasis adhesive
- Moss
- Bent wire pins (optional)
- 4 short-stemmed, white moth orchids, with folilage attached
- 4 plant stakes
- Raffia or floral wire

1

Fill your container with Oasis foam, cutting it to fit if necessary. Secure it in place using the adhesive. Then arrange some moss over the top so that all the foam is concealed. Insert bent wire pins to hold the moss in place, if desired. Alternatively, secure the moss with a little Oasis adhesive.

2

Set the container in front of you so one corner faces forward. Push one orchid into the Oasis toward the opposite corner, at the back of the display. Angle the blooms to lean out toward the right. Push another orchid into the foam just in front and slightly to the left of the first orchid. Stand this one upright.

3

Take another orchid and push this into the foam at the corner of the container that faces the front. Angle the flower head so it faces out and slightly to the left. Add the remaining orchid to the right of the last one, with the flowers angled out and to the right.

4

Push a plant stake into the foam next to the last orchid added. Use raffia or floral wire to secure the flower stem to the stake. Repeat to secure the other orchids to the remaining plant stakes.

Design ideas

The simplicity of this design means that you can easily substitute different colored blooms. Deep magenta or pale green orchids would work just as well. Make sure you pick a plain, unadorned container if you want a display that will suit any room or decorative style.

CHAPTER 3

Create with Color

From subtle shades to brilliant hues, the range of colors you can find in faux flowers is astonishing. Whether you decide on a multicolored or a monochromatic display, you're sure to find a color that suits any mood or complements any setting.

GLORIOUS COLOR

The beautiful big blooms of traditional English roses are a fleeting pleasure in nature, but in silk they last forever. Create this colorful display of dark pink and multicolored roses and you'll have a stunning arrangement that you can enjoy all year-round.

You will need

- Black cube-shaped acrylic or glass vase, about 10 in (25 cm) square
- 24 yellow-and-pink English roses
- 9 dark pink English roses
- Raffia or floral wire

1 —————————————

Take six of the yellow-and-pink roses and two of the dark pink roses and trim the stems to about 8 in (20 cm) long. Retain any leaves that are close to the flower head but remove any further down the stem. Gather together the yellow-and-pink roses into a loose bunch, then add the dark pink ones at the bottom and to one side of the bunch. Tie with raffia or floral wire.

2 —————————————

Take six more yellow-and-pink roses and two more dark pink roses and make into a bunch in the same way. Repeat with the remaining yellow-and-pink roses and four more dark pink ones to make two more bunches. Trim the stems on all the bunches so that they are level.

Design ideas

English roses have blooms that are made up of many loose petals. The multicolored varieties, like the yellow-and-pink ones used here, can be formed of petals in several different shades, allowing you to introduce a depth of color and detail into a display with the use of just one flower type.

3 —————————————

Place two of the bunches in the vase at the front. Arrange the bunches so the dark pink roses are lower and touch the edge of the container.

4 —————————————

Add the remaining two bunches at the back of the container. Adjust the four bunches so that they overhang the edge of the container in a pleasing way. Take the remaining dark pink rose and insert this at the very center of the display to conceal any gap between the bunches.

GRAND GESTURE

When you want to be creative with color but don't want to mix and match too many different shades, it's a great idea to pick a single strong hue as your focal point. The deep velvety purple of these Vanda orchids is truly eye-catching.

You will need

- Rectangular glass vase, about 20 in (50 cm) tall and 12 in (30 cm) wide
- Oasis foam
- Oasis adhesive
- Moss
- Knitting needle
- 4 purple Vanda orchids
- 2 clumps of Vanda orchid leaves

1 ————————————

Fill the bottom of the vase to just under half way up with some Oasis foam, leaving a gap of about 3/8 in (1 cm) all around the sides. Secure it in place with Oasis adhesive. Take some moss and, using a knitting needle, push it between the Oasis and the sides of the vase to conceal the foam. Cover the Oasis at the top with more moss.

2 ————————————

Take one clump of leaves and push it into the foam just to the right of center and slightly toward the back. Add the other clump of leaves just to the left of center and slightly toward the front. For added security, dab a little Oasis glue on the ends of the stems before pushing them into the foam.

Design ideas

The supporting medium in this display is Oasis foam, hidden from view at the sides of the glass vase by masking it with moss. If you want, you could substitute the foam with decorative pebbles. Fill the vase to at least one-third, and push the stems in between the pebbles for support.

3 ————————————

Take one of the orchids and push the stem into the foam, close to the first clump of leaves. Arrange the flower head so it leans outward and toward the back right of the display. Push another orchid into the foam, close to the second clump of leaves. Angle this bloom to lean toward the back left of the display.

4 ————————————

Take the two remaining orchids and push their stems into the foam, close to the first two flowers, with one facing out to the front left and one facing out to the front right. Push the stems of these flowers deeper into the foam so that the flower heads are at a lower level than the first two orchids.

PRETTY IN PINK

A contrast in shapes and textures is the key to this display's design success. Big, bold, and bright pink, the ring of roses bursts from a mound of delicate purple wild agapanthus flowers. The circular arrangement looks good from any angle.

You will need

- Shallow cylindrical glass vase, about 6 in (15 cm) tall and 10 in (25 cm) in diameter
- Oasis foam
- Oasis adhesive
- 3–4 aspidistra leaves
- 8–10 deep purple wild agapanthus clumps, divided into about 30 smaller clumps
- 7 bright pink old roses

1

Fill your container with Oasis foam, leaving a small gap between the foam and the sides of the vase; glue it in place. Slip the aspidistra leaves in between the Oasis and the sides of the vase, making sure the leaves overlap and conceal the foam. Take about 10 of the agapanthus clumps and push them into the center of the foam to form a tight bunch.

2

Take the remaining agapanthus clumps and push them into the Oasis around the edge of the container. Angle the blooms so they lean outward from the center. There should be a gap between the central clump of agapanthus and the outer ring.

Design ideas

Although the overall shape of this arrangement is neat and symmetrical, it still relies on contrasts to create impact. If you want to change the flowers used, maintain this design dynamic and combine large, solid-shaped blooms – like roses, lilies, and peonies – with smaller, frothy flowers – such as clematis, cow parsley, or lady's mantle.

3

Take one of the roses and push it into the foam, between the central clump of wild agapanthus flowers and the outer ring of flowers. Push the stem in so that the rose bloom is level with the top of the wild agapanthus flowers. Trim the rose stems if necessary. Start adding more roses.

4

Use the remaining roses to fill the gap between the central clump of wild agapanthus and the outer ring. Space the roses evenly so there are no gaps in between the flowers.

BEAUTIFUL BLUES

The stately spires of delphinium flower heads are made up of a mass of smaller frilly blooms with petals in subtle shades of blue, grouped around a tiny, white, star-like center. Blue-grey eucalyptus leaves make the perfect partner for a serene yet splendid display.

You will need

- Large ceramic vase, about 10 in (25 cm) tall, with a narrow neck, about 4 in (10 cm) across
- Oasis foam
- Oasis adhesive
- 2 short eucalyptus branches, about 10 in (25 cm) long
- 9 light blue delphiniums
- 2 long eucalyptus branches, about 36 in (1 m) long
- 4–6 medium length eucalyptus branches, 16–20 in (40–50 cm) long

1

Fill your container with Oasis foam so that the top of the foam is level with the top of the vase neck; secure with some Oasis glue. Take one of the short eucalyptus branches and push it into the foam at the left of the vase. Push the other short eucalyptus branch into the foam at the right. Angle both branches so they fall downward over either side of the container.

2

Take one delphinium and push it into the foam at the center. These are rather top-heavy flowers, so it's a good idea to put a dab of Oasis glue on the end of the stem before pushing it into the foam. Let this flower stand tall and straight; this delphinium forms the highest point in the display.

3

Take a second delphinium and push it into the foam at an angle to the right of the first flower. Push another delphinium in at an angle to the left. Push the stems a bit deeper into the foam so the flower heads are slightly lower than the first flower.

4

Push another delphinium into the foam just in front of the center flower, angling the stem so the flower head falls out and slightly forward. Push another delphinium into the foam just behind the right-hand flower, angling the stem so it leans further out toward the right.

Design ideas

Although delphiniums are typical cottage-garden plants, they aren't cottage-garden size. Their tall stature and long flower spikes – which make them ideal for the back of the flower border – mean they are ideal statement blooms. They are perfect for when you want to design a large display made up of a single type.

Sylvia says...

Blue can be quite a tricky color when it comes to arranging flowers. In color theory, it's what is known as a receding color. This means that when you look at a group of objects, the blue things will appear to be further away, or to recede. Anything that's a dominant color, like red or orange, will appear to be further forward than the blue items. This means, of course, that when you put together an arrangement that includes a mix of colors, the blue flowers will recede into the background somewhat. So, what do you do if you want to make blue the main color? Well, the simplest answer is to make blue the only flower color you use! The delphiniums I've chosen for this display are such magnificent blooms that it would be a shame if they became just "filler flowers". By combining them with the cool, blue-green eucalyptus foliage, I've made sure that it's the delphiniums that are the real focus here.

5

Now push another delphinium into the foam, just to the right of the central flower, so that it angles out to the right. Push another flower in at the left-hand side, between the two flowers that are already there, and then add the last flower, at the center front. Angle the stems on these last two so their flowers point outward.

6

Take one of the long eucalyptus branches and push it into the foam at the back of the display, to the right of the central flower. Add the other long eucalyptus branch to the left of the center. Push the stems of both in so that they are only just a little shorter than the central flower. These foliage stems should lean away from the center slightly.

7

Now take the medium-length eucalyptus branches and start adding them at the front of the display. You are aiming to fill any gaps between the flowers and existing foliage, and to obscure the foam from view. Push the stems in so that the eucalyptus branches fall outward and forward over the edge of the vase, and so they are longer than the first two pieces of foliage added at step 1.

STRIKE A POSE

If you want to put on a real show, why not try this truly bold arrangement? Combine opulent magenta orchids with the strong architectural shapes of twisted willow stems, and raise the curtain on a dramatic masterpiece.

You will need

- Rounded glass vase, wider at the top than at the bottom, about 16 in (40 cm) tall and about 8 in (20 cm) diameter at the neck
- Grey decorative pebbles
- 2 twisted willow stems
- 4 large spotted magenta moth orchids

1

Gradually add pebbles to the vase until it is about one-third full. Do this by taking a small handful of pebbles and putting your hand right to the bottom of the vase before letting go. Build up the pebbles in layers in this way until you have the required amount. Don't drop them all in at once or you might break or scratch the glass vase.

2

Take one twisted willow stem and put it into the vase on the right-hand side. Push it gently into the pebbles to hold it in place; the stem should rest on the right-hand side of the vase, with the twists at the top leaning slightly to the right. Put the remaining twisted willow in at the left-hand side, with the twists at the top facing to the left.

3

Take two of the orchids and push them into the pebbles near the front of the display, with the ends of the stems fairly close together. Allow both flowers to lean back against the willow stems so the blooms are supported by the twists. Arrange them so one flower leans out to the left, and one leans out to the right.

4

Take another orchid and push it into the pebbles slightly to the left of the left-hand flower. Place the remaining orchid slightly to the right of the right-hand flower. Push the stems a bit further into the pebbles so these flowers are at a lower level. Let them lean forward, so the stems rest on the edge of the vase.

Design ideas

Twisted willow stems have been used to create an interesting background for the magenta moth orchids in this display, rather than a more traditional spray of foliage. The strongly delineated shapes of the willow stems form graphic outlines around the softer shapes of the drooping flower heads.

BOLD STATEMENT

When you are choosing the different elements for a successful faux-flower display, you want to pick blooms that are suitably showy. These dahlias, with their rich wine-red tones, are the ideal choice for a stunning arrangement that's big on character.

You will need

- Shallow rectangular glass vase, about 12 in (30 cm) tall, 10 in (25 cm) wide and 3 in (7.5 cm) deep
- 6 magnolia branches, between 10 in (25 cm) and 20 in (50 cm) in length
- 2 long vine tendrils
- 9 dark red dahlias, with buds and foliage attached

1

Take two of the magnolia branches and place them in the vase so the ends are roughly in the center. Arrange them so one branch leans left and one leans right; they will form a rough V shape. Add a short branch at the right-hand side of the vase, making sure it leans slightly rather than stands upright.

2

Take another magnolia branch and place it in the vase toward the front, with its end touching the end of the last branch added and the top leaning toward the left. Add two more branches toward the back, with their ends at the back left of the vase and leaning out toward the right.

Design ideas

Dahlias come in various colors, usually shades of red, orange, yellow, and pink. The deep wine-red of the dahlias used here is a particularly dramatic color and works well with the dark wood of the magnolia branches. You could create a brighter display by using lighter colored flowers.

3

Take one of the vine tendrils and place it in the vase so the end is just to the right of center and the tendril leans to the right. If the tendril has two branches, arrange it so the tallest branch is the one leaning to the right.

4

Add two dahlias to the vase. Place one so its end is at the right-hand side of the vase and the flower head leans to the left, with the stem resting on the vase edge. Place the other so it leans out toward the right, with the stem resting on the edge of the vase.

5

Take two more dahlias and add these to the vase so that the ends of their stems touch the bottom of the vase at roughly left of center. The stems should lean to the right and the flower heads should be facing toward the right.

6

Take another dahlia and add to the vase so the end of the stem touches the bottom of the vase at the left-hand side. The stem should lean into the center of the display, with the flower facing up and slightly to the right. Add another in roughly the same place, with the stem leaning toward the center and the flower facing upward.

7

Add two dahlias at the back of the display, with one leaning to the right and one to the left. The flower heads should face slightly toward the back of the display. Add the last dahlia at the center back with the stem fairly upright and the flower head turning slightly toward the back. Slip the remaining vine tendril into the arrangement at the right-hand side, turning the stem so that the twisting tendril reaches toward the left of the display.

SHOCKING PINK

For a real hot blast of color, go for a pink that's nearly neon in its brightness. These magnificent moth orchids are the ideal shade of brilliant pink, and this simple yet graphically strong display is sure to attract lots of attention.

You will need

- Black cube-shaped acrylic or glass vase, about 10 in (25 cm) square
- Oasis foam (optional)
- 4 tied clumps of meadow grass
- 3 bright pink moth orchids

1

Take one of the clumps of meadow grass and place it into the container at the back left corner. Push it well into the corner so it stands tall and upright, supported by the sides of the vase. Take another clump of grass and place it in the back right corner in the same way.

2

Take the two remaining clumps of meadow grass and put these into the front left and front right corners. The grass clumps need to sit fairly tightly in the vase, so if necessary you can use a block of Oasis foam to wedge them in place – push it in between the grass at the center. Take one orchid and push it down into the grass clump in the back left corner.

3

Take a second orchid and trim about 1 in (2.5 cm) off the end of the stem. Push this orchid among the leaves of the front right clump of meadow grass. Make sure the flowers are angled so they face toward the front.

4

Trim about 2 in (5 cm) off the end of the stem of the remaining orchid. Push this flower in among the leaves of the front left clump of meadow grass. Turn the stem so the flowers face to the front left of the display.

Sylvia says...

These faux-flower moth orchids have a tendency to droop forward if the stems are left unsupported. Now, generally speaking, I like to exploit a flower's natural tendency and would usually create a display that allowed the moth orchids to fall outward. But for this arrangement I needed to design something that was more upright, more linear in look. The clumps of meadow grass were ideal for adding a strong vertical element and, at the same time, they acted as plant stakes: the moth orchid stems were slipped in among the grass clumps and were held by them in an upright position.

COUNTRY CHARM

There's nothing like a mass of flowers for creating an impression, and an armful of pretty pansies and lovely lavender makes the ideal filling for this unusual container. The deep, dusky purple of the pansies is perfectly complemented by the lighter hues of the lavender.

You will need

- Large metal bucket-like container, about 14 in (35 cm) tall and 12 in (30 cm) wide at the opening, with attached candle holders
- Oasis foam
- Oasis adhesive
- Moss
- Bent wire pins (optional)
- 5 large clumps of lavender
- 7 sprigs of dark purple pansies
- Four candles

1

Fill your chosen container with Oasis foam (see "Sylvia says..." below) and secure with glue. Arrange some moss over the top of the Oasis so that all the foam is concealed. Use bent wire pins or glue to hold the moss in place. Push two clumps of lavender into the foam at the back of the container, angling the stems so they lean slightly outward.

2

Take another lavender clump and push it into the container at the very front, angling it so the flower stems lean out toward the front. Add another lavender clump to the right of this, and another to the left. Gently tweak the lavender leaves and stems so there are no gaps between the clumps. There should be a slight gap at the very center of the display.

Sylvia says...

The container I chose for this display is quite deep, so I didn't want to completely fill it with Oasis foam as this would be quite costly. To get around the problem, I found a cheap, plastic flower pot that was about half the height of my chosen container and that, when turned upside down, fitted inside perfectly. I then only had to add Oasis to fill half the container.

The container also features an integral candle holder for four candles. If you are using a similar container, do be careful when lighting the candles and angle the flames away from the flowers.

3

Take one pansy sprig and push it into the center, angling the stem toward the back. Add two more clumps at the center, positioning each so the flowers lean outward.

4

Now use the remaining pansy sprigs to fill in around the outside of the display. Depending on the size of your container, you may need to divide the sprigs up into smaller parts to give you enough to fill all around. Angle the stems so that the flowers lean outward.

CHAPTER 4

Faux Flower Know-how

It's easy to shape and adapt faux flowers in order to create almost any style of arrangement; all you need are a few tools and some basic techniques. With an understanding of some simple design principles, you can put together almost any display you want.

DESIGN BASICS

If you grabbed a handful of faux flowers and then dropped them in a vase, you would be very lucky if the result was pleasing. It takes a little time and consideration to create a successful arrangement, and you need to follow a few design rules. Fortunately, these rules are easy to master.

When you are designing a faux flower display, your first consideration should be where the arrangement will be positioned. If your vase is going to be placed on a table or other piece of furniture where you will be able to see it from every angle, then the display needs to look as good from the back as it does from the front. If, on the other hand, the flowers are to be set against a wall, then the design will be seen only from the front and sides. The exception to this is if you position your arrangment in front of a mirror.

Very simply speaking, faux flower arrangements are either symmetrical or asymmetrical in their design. In a symmetrical arrangement there is an imaginary line that divides the display in two, and the elements to the left of this line will be mirrored on the right. In an asymmetrical display the elements to the left of the imaginary line are not mirrored on the opposite side. There are, of course, many exceptions to these rules! You may create an arrangement that is symmetrical in its shape but introduces an element of asymmetry in the colors used. For example, after adding a red flower at the bottom left of the vase, you can place another red flower at the top right rather than mirroring the first red flower with a matching bloom at the bottom right.

It's also worth noting that it's hard to create a truly symmetrical display. It's nearly impossible to arrange flowers so

This carefully composed display is a masterpiece of design. The asymmetric arrangement of the alliums is perfectly balanced by the curving lines of the water lily leaves and stems.

as to form a perfect mirror image on either side of the display, and flowers, both faux and real, are seldom identical.

When you're creating a symmetrical arrangement, the imaginary dividing line in the display is usually – but not always – a vertical one that runs through the center of the design. In an arrangement that's to be seen in the round, this imaginary line would run through the very center of the vase; in an arrangement that's set against a wall, the line would run through the center back. For a balanced arrangement, the tallest element should be aligned with this central line: you can place the tallest flower at dead center, as in "Beautiful Blues" on page 64, or you can place your tallest stems on either side of the center line, as in "Thoroughly Modern" on page 28.

Even if you're not aiming for perfect symmetry, this imaginary center line is still invaluable. As you place flowers

in your arrangement, you can position them so they lean outward and away from the center line, as in "Grace and Splendor" on page 49.

There are other lines in your faux flower displays that are just as important. The stems of your flowers and foliage create lines in your design, and these need to follow a strong framework if the finished arrangement is to please the eye. These design lines can fan out from a fixed point (or points), can criss-cross, or can run parallel to one another. For example, in "Pretty in Pink" on page 62, the flower stems all fan out from a central point somewhere in the middle of the vase; in "Bold Statement" on page 69, stark branches criss-cross inside the vase in contrast with the texture of the flowers used; and in "Making an Entrance" on page 17, plant stakes are used to add a strong vertical element that complements the graceful droop of the orchids.

SYMMETRY

If you're creating a truly symmetrical display, you will be trying to exactly match one side of the arrangement to the other. A flower placed on the right of the display will have its matching bloom on the left (as in "Pure and Bright", page 40 and right). You can still, however, use symmetry in a display without one side being a mirror image of the other. If you establish the center line of your arrangement, you can use the same amount of flowers and stems on either side of this line to make a display that is perfecly balanced, if not perfectly symmetrical (as in "Magnificent Magnolias", page 20, and right).

ASYMMETRY

If you are putting together an asymmetrical design, you won't be trying to evenly balance the elements on both sides of the display. You may have more of one flower type on one side, for example. Or the flowers and branches may droop down on the left-hand side, but not on the right, for example (as in "Strike a Pose", page 67 and left). Even though such an arrangement is not symmetrical, you will still be working with an imaginary axis – which may or may not be at the center. Your flowers and branches have to lean away from something, so you need a fixed point in the display.

COLOR THEORY

Color theory is used by artists and designers to help them comprehend how colors work. An understanding of the visual impact different colors can have is invaluable when it comes to making creative decisions, and you can use this understanding when choosing the ingredients for your faux flower displays.

The color wheel (see opposite) is a diagram that helps illustrate color theory. On it you will see the three primary colors – red, yellow and blue; these are the colors from which all other colors are mixed. Between the primary colors you will see the three secondary colors – orange, violet, and green. Each of these is created by mixing together two primary colors – orange is made by mixing yellow and red so it is placed between these two on the color wheel; violet and green are positioned between the two colors from which they are made. The six tertiary colors are created by mixing the primary and secondary colors next to each other on the color wheel – so a yellow-orange is made by mixing yellow with orange, a blue-green is created from blue mixed with green, and so on.

The point of arranging primary, secondary, and tertiary colors on a wheel is that you can see how they relate to each other. The colors opposite each other on the wheel are complementary colors. Red and green, yellow and violet, and blue and orange are complementary pairs, but so are yellow-orange and blue-violet – they are all directly opposite each other on the color wheel. Complementary colors are also often known as constrasting colors because, put simply, they clash when placed next to each other. But this clash creates a visual interest – one that you can exploit when choosing flower combinations.

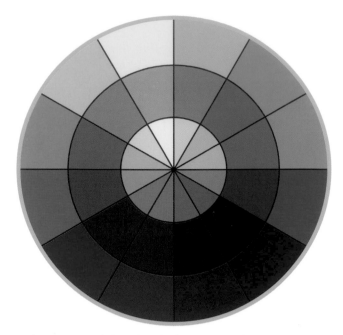

On the outer ring of this color wheel you can see the primary colors – red, yellow, and blue – with the secondary and tertiary colors in between. If you mix black with any color you produce a shade; if you mix in white you will get a tint of that color. The shades of each color are shown on the middle ring of the color wheel; the tints are shown on the inner ring.

MONOCHROMATIC SCHEMES

If you opt for a monochromatic color scheme, you will be working with just one color. You can, however, use the shades and tints of that color.

COMPLEMENTARY SCHEMES

A complementary scheme has colors opposite each other on the wheel. In "Shocking Pink" (see page 72), the orchids are a tint of reddish violet, and opposite a yellow-green on the wheel.

HARMONIC SCHEMES

In a harmonic scheme you need to use two or three colors next to each other on the color wheel: "Pretty in Pink" (see page 62) uses pinks and violets.

ESSENTIAL SUPPORTS

There are certain times when you may need to add some kind of support
to your silk flower arrangements in order to hold the blooms in just the right position,
and there are a variety of easy-to-use options available.

When you're putting together an arrangement of faux flowers, some, but not all, designs will need the addition of a support medium. Most commonly, this will be floral foam, which is usually known by its trademark name, Oasis, but you can also use decorative pebbles and sand. Plant stakes, to which you can secure flower stems, and various ties and tape will also be handy.

One of the great advantages of faux flowers is that you don't have to put water in the vase, so you don't need to use a watertight container. This means you can use virtually anything as a container for your display. The only disadvantage to this is if you choose a particularly lightweight container, such as a woven basket or tin – the weight of your flowers might cause the whole display to topple over. This is where a support medium comes into play.

When pushed into Oasis foam, the stem of a faux flower is held tightly in place. If your container is tightly packed with foam, you have a more secure base for your display. Oasis can also be glued inside the container for added security; you can use specialist Oasis adhesive or a hot glue gun to do this. It's also possible to apply the same adhesive to the end of a faux flower stem before pushing it into the foam; this holds the flower in place even more firmly.

Decorative pebbles and sand can also be added to a container to give support to faux flower stems. All you need to do is put a layer of the pebbles or sand in the bottom of the vase and then push in the flowers. Care must be taken when adding these to glass containers, since they might scratch or even break a fragile vase.

Another way to ensure your faux flower display will stay in place is to use plant stakes. After pushing a faux flower into the floral foam, you can push in a suitable stake close to the stem and then tie the flower to the stake.

Some faux flowers have fairly long stems and, over time, the weight of the flower heads could cause them to bend or droop. If you're using long-stemmed blooms, consider using some plant stakes for a bit of extra support. The flower stems are simply tied to the stakes with raffia, twine, or floral wire.

FLORAL FOAM

Oasis foam comes in a wide range of shapes and sizes. Square and rectangular blocks are probably the most useful, but you'll also find spheres and cones for sale. There are also foam shapes designed for certain display types – you can buy foam shapes for wreaths, bouquets, and garlands. When shopping for Oasis, look for dry floral foam, intended for use in arrangements that don't need water. If you can't find a block to fit your chosen container, it is possible to cut Oasis into new shapes. Use a sharp knife, preferably one with a serrated blade, and simply slice into the foam. It's a good idea to wear a face mask if you are cutting up lots of foam; minute granules of the foam fall off as you cut into it, and these may irritate if inhaled. You could also wear latex gloves to keep the foam particles off your hands.

DECORATIVE PEBBLES AND SAND

An interesting alternative to Oasis foam is using something more decorative, something that looks good by itself. Decorative pebbles and sand are ideal for this; they fill all or part of the vase, and the faux flowers are simply pushed in. The stems are held in place between the pebbles or grains of sand. They are also useful since their weight can help prevent a vase with a top-heavy arrangement from falling over. Because they are decorative features, the pebbles and sand should be used with clear or opaque containers, where they can be seen through the sides. If your vase is glass, don't ever pour in the stones or sand – there's always the possibility that they may break the glass. Instead, take a handful of stones or sand and put your hand in the vase, right to the bottom. Let go of the pebbles or sand so they settle gently in the vase. Continue in this way until you have enough in your vase. Take the same precautions with acrylic containers since they can also be scratched by the pebbles or sand.

MOSS

The downside of using Oasis foam is that it's not particularly attractive. When you've filled your chosen container with Oasis, you may want to conceal the top of the foam. It may be that the display you intend to create will be of such a size and arrangement that the flowers and foliage will completely cover the top of the vase, and if this is the case then you shouldn't worry. If, however, there is any possibility that the top of the Oasis foam will be visible, then you can use moss to cover it. Simply arrange the moss over the top and use bent wire pins to hold it in place. The pins look like elongated staples, and they are pushed through the moss and into the foam. Alternatively, you can apply a few dabs of Oasis adhesive to the top of the foam and stick the moss down on these. Both real and artificial moss is available.

FAUX FOLIAGE

More often than not, faux flowers come with foliage attached. You can also buy separate sprays of foliage. Some leaves are particularly large, and these can be put to good use by adding as a decorative element to your glass containers. Because Oasis foam does not look good on its own, it's not ideal when you want to use a glass container – the foam can be seen through the clear sides of the vase. However, you can use a large faux leaf to conceal the foam. All you need to do is cut the foam so there's a slight gap between it and the sides of the vase, and then slip some larger leaves into the gap. You will need a few leaves since they will have to overlap, but you could also cut them into smaller sections to fill any spaces. Ideal leaves to use for this are aspidistra (see right), anthurium, water lily, and hydrangea.

STAKES AND TIES

There are a variety of different stakes available to use in faux flower displays. Suppliers of equipment specifically for artificial flower arrangements will stock plant stakes, but you can also try the stakes that are used to support house plants. If your display is particularly large, then the canes used for garden plants might well be suitable. Pick a stake that goes with your flowers and the design of your display. Thin, spindly supports will look odd when combined with thick-stemmed flowers, just as thick, knobbly twigs won't go with delicate, fine blooms.

If you use stakes to support blooms, you will need something with which to tie everything together. Raffia is a useful option: it's inexpensive and comes in a variety of colors, and the natural look of undyed raffia means it works well with virtually any faux flower. Garden twine is another excellent tie, Available in green or string color, it's an unobtrusive tie and is useful if you don't want to make a feature of the plant stakes.

You can also use floral wire to secure flower stems to stakes; the wire can be twisted around the flower and then around the stake. Floral wire is available either covered or uncovered – the covered type is usually wrapped with green plastic. Wire has other uses: you can wrap it around the stems of flowers and then bend it, which is ideal if you want to manipulate your chosen blooms into different shapes. Wire, raffia, and twine can also be used to tie flowers into bunches, practically or decoratively.

And lastly there is floral tape. This low-tack tape can be used to bind stems to stakes, and to tie flowers into bunches, but it is most useful for repairs (see page 86).

ACRYLIC WATER

This support medium is used when you want to create a display that appears to be set in water. It is created by mixing together two chemical substances; this is poured into a vase and then the faux flowers are arranged before the mixture sets. A display that uses this artificial water needs to be set aside for up to 48 hours while the resin sets solid. Once it's set, it's nearly impossible to remove the acrylic water, so you should only use it with a container that you have no desire to use again.

Acrylic water should be used very carefully; the two substances combined to make it are highly toxic. Always follow the manufacturer's instructions and read any of the cautionary notes that come with the different substances. You will need suitable protection for your hands and eyes, and something disposable in which to mix the resin.

Try to work out how much acrylic water you need before you start, and only mix up that amount. Never pour unused acrylic-water products down the sink or into your drainage system – it will set solid and cause a blockage. If you do make up too much of the mixture, pour the unwanted resin into an old tin or plastic pot, and leave the acrylic to set before disposing of both safely.

ESSENTIAL TECHNIQUES

Faux flowers are very easy to work with, and the techniques required are easy to master.
Silk flowers are also very forgiving and can stand up to a fair amount of wear and tear. That said,
there are a few useful tips for getting the best out of your blooms.

More often that not, when you are putting together a display of silk flowers, you will have to alter or manipulate the flowers in some way. This can mean simply bending the stems into shape – and this is quite easy since many faux flowes have wired stems – or it can mean cutting into stems or branches.

In most displays, there will be some flowers or branches of foliage that are longer than others. The elements that you use to add height or width in an arrangement will have the longest stems, and you may not have to reduce their length at all. But as you build up a display you will start adding shorter flowers, and to get these just right you will probably have to trim off some of the stem. Because most faux flowers have wire at the heart of their stems, you will need wire cutters for the job. Ordinary wire cutters should be perfectly suitable, but you might want to invest in speciality cutters, especially if you plan to work with faux flowers on a regular basis.

Many faux flowers are made up of several smaller branches or stems, and there are times when you want to divide up one flowering stem into smaller elements. You may want to make the most of flowers that come in a clump by dividing them up into lots of smaller clumps. Or you might want to cut a flower with mulitple stems down to a more suitable size. You might even want to remove all or part of the foliage. With some faux flowers, especially those made up of many smaller flower heads, the individual stems do not have wire in them, so these are easily cut with ordinary scissors. Otherwise, you can use wire cutters to divide up faux flowers.

Occasionally, you may need to join together parts of faux flowers; you might want to reattach a leaf or petal that's fallen off, or you might want to add extra petals to bulk out a silk flower. If you do, then the best tool to use is a hot glue gun. A solid glue stick is heated in the glue gun until it liquifies; this is then applied through the nozzle of the gun.

The short, cylindrical glass vase used for this display called for an arrangement of tightly packed flowers. Peonies were the ideal choice, but these large flowers have long stems and it was necessary to trim them to a much shorter length.

The adhesive is very strong, and using a nozzle means that you can be very accurate in placing the glue exactly where you want it. If you decide to use a hot glue gun, always follow the manufacturer's advice on usage, wear protective gloves, and work in a well-ventilated room.

Before you start work on a display, you should inspect the flowers carefully, even if they're brand new. If the petals or leaves have been crushed or folded, you can usually just reshape them with your fingers. If the creases are stubborn, however, you can steam them out. Boil water in a teapot and then hold the flower head in the jet of steam coming from the spout for a few seconds. Remove the flower from the steam and use your fingertips to smooth out any creases or wrinkles in the petals and leaves. You can use the same technique with flower heads that are too tightly packed: hold them over the steam and then tease the petals apart with your fingers.

Faux flowers do gather dust, and the best way to deal with this is regular cleaning. You can use a soft cloth to wipe larger leaves and petals, but for smaller elements and hard-to-reach areas you can use a hair dryer (set on cool) or a can of compressed air to blow away dust.

If you are reusing flowers from an older display, you may need to do a bit of renovation and repair. This might be as simple as trimming away any loose or frayed bits of silk from the edges of petals or leaves; in this instance, a pair of small scissors will be ideal for the job. Stems can break sometimes, but, generally speaking, these can be easily spliced back together using floral tape (see below and page 84).

You can also give your flowers a whole new life with fabric dye and paint. White and other pale-colored blooms can be dyed to a darker color and hand-painted details can be added to enhance the form of the flower (see opposite page).

MENDING FAUX FLOWERS

You can join together a broken stem by using floral tape. Start by wrapping some tape tightly around one part of the broken stem to secure it. Bring the two broken ends together and hold them in place while you continue to wrap the tape around the stem. Take the tape right along the stem, well past the break. To finish, cut off the tape and smooth the cut end tightly against the wrapped section.

DYEING FAUX FLOWERS

Silk flowers are easy to dye; look for dyes specifically for silk.Choose a dye that's mixed with cold water, since silk may not react well to hot water. Pale colored flowers will work best with dye. Mix the dye according to the manufacturer's instructions, but start with a stronger concentration than recommended. Start by using this concentrated solution to make a weak dye bath. You can strengthen the solution until you get the result you want. It is better to start with something too light since you can darken it, but you won't be able to lighten a color that is too dark. You can add detail to dyed flowers by hand-painting them. Use a strong concentration of the dye or a suitable fabric paint, and add some delicate shading to the petals with an artist's paint brush.

1 Mix up your chosen dye to a fairly strong concentration, following the manufacturer's instructions. Set aside a small amount of the concentrated dye if you want to do any hand-painting at a later stage (see step 5). Pour a small amount of the concentrated dye into a glass bowl or plastic pot and then dilute with water. You want to start with a fairly weak color.

2 The stems of some faux flowers may be made of a material that absorbs the dye. To be on the safe side, tightly wrap some plastic wrap around the stem from right below the flower head to the end.

3 Immerse your flower head in the diluted dye solution (see step 1). Hold it in for a few seconds and then lift out to check the color. If it is lighter that you want, put it back in the dye for a bit longer. Alternatively, mix a bit more of the concentrated dye into the bowl so you have a stronger dye bath.

4 Make a pile of several pieces of paper towels or use an old, clean towel; set the dyed flower on top to dry. When it's completely dry check the shade. If you want it darker dip it in the dye again. If you want to add any hand-painted details, go on to step 5.

5 You can hand-paint detail on a dyed flower. Use the concentrated dye solution that you set aside at step 1 (or fabric paint) and a small artist's paint brush. Apply the dye along the edges and any raised area of the petals. Be subtle and build up the color very gradually for a natural effect.

CHAPTER 5

Faux Flower Spectrum

From the deepest, dark purple shades to the brightest, purest white, there is a rainbow range of colors available in faux flowers. Take your pick from this comprehensive directory of stunning silk blooms to find the ideal flowers for your particular arrangement.

FAUX FLOWER SPECTRUM

When you are putting together a faux flower display, you first need to choose your color palette. Once you've selected your key bloom (or blooms), you need to decide which other flowers and foliage to add to the mix. Do you go for a contrast in colors, or for a dramatic play between light and dark? Or do you stick to one color only and build up a monochromatic masterpiece? The pages that follow give you a guide to different colors of both faux flowers and foliage, as well as an idea of their impact and ideal uses.

DEEP PURPLE PARROT TULIP

FLOWERS The petals have a deeply fringed edge and a slightly ruffled texture, in contrast to the smooth, glossy petals of standard tulips.

LEAVES & STEMS Thick, upright stems; the two long leaves are wrapped around the base of the stem

SIZE & IMPACT Each stems bears one flower head, about 4 in (15 cm) long and wide.

PERFECT FOR ... Arrangements that mix different colored tulips, both standard and parrot.

BEECH LEAVES

FLOWERS Flowerless.

LEAVES & STEMS Several twiggy branches emerge from the main stem. Each branch bears plenty of purple leaves that are tinged with green.

SIZE & IMPACT Tall stems with several branches that can be spread out. The leaves are about 2 in (5 cm) long.

PERFECT FOR ... Combining with foliage stems that have greener leaves to create shadow and depth; combine with flowers in similar shades or in a contrasting greenish yellow.

WINE-RED DAHLIA

FLOWERS Each bloom is made up of many petals, tightly packed at the center. Stems include neat buds, with a few petals emerging at the end.

LEAVES & STEMS Strong, upright stems. The mid-green leaves are oval with serrated edges.

SIZE & IMPACT Medium- to large-sized flowers, about 5 in (12.5 cm) across.

PERFECT FOR ... Grouping together to make the most of the intense color, or combining with lime-green blooms.

BURGUNDY RANUNCULUS

FLOWERS Blooms with many circular, overlapping petals in a deep burgundy-red color. The flowers look like roses on the point of opening.

LEAVES & STEMS Thick, erect stems with a few feathery, pale green leaves borne where the flowering stems divide.

SIZE & IMPACT Two flowers to each stem, about 2 in (5 cm) wide, occasionally with a small bud attached.

PERFECT FOR ... Adding an accent color in a display, particularly if a deeper shade is required.

DEEP PINK OLD ROSE

FLOWERS A traditional, old-fashioned style of rose in an intense bright pink. Many loose, soft petals are clustered around golden yellow stamens.

LEAVES & STEMS Slender stems with a few small leaves near the flower head.

SIZE & IMPACT Flowers held singly or in pairs, with second bloom partially opened.

PERFECT FOR ... Making an impact; any display where you want a distinct area in a deep, bright color.

PINK AMARYLLIS

FLOWERS Large, open flowers with big, fleshy petals in a deep magenta streaked with white. Long, curling, white stamens at the center.

LEAVES & STEMS Very thick, upright, fleshy stems without any leaves.

SIZE & IMPACT Large, exotic-looking flowers, each about 6 in (15 cm) across.

PERFECT FOR ... Modern, minimal displays, using a few single blooms, or grouped together in an impressive mass.

MAGENTA MOTH ORCHID

FLOWERS Outer petals of magenta, fading to pink and then white at the center. Small inner petals in the same shade of pink, held around a pale green center.

LEAVES & STEMS Tall, slender stems with flowers held on smaller stems at the top. Long, thick, fleshy leaves and pale, grey-green aerial roots at the base of the stems.

SIZE & IMPACT Six to eight flowers, about 2 in (5 cm) wide, on each stem, plus several buds.

PERFECT FOR ... Using alone or in groups of matching orchids.

DEEP PINK PEONY

FLOWERS Large, cup-shaped flower with wide, circular outer petals and narrower, smaller inner petals in an intense shade of deep magenta pink.

LEAVES & STEMS Slim, upright stems with light green, slightly veined, spear-shaped leaves.

SIZE & IMPACT Flowers of about 5 in (12.5 cm) in width are held on the top of stems.

PERFECT FOR ... Combining with other pink or purple flowers; ideal as the focal point in such displays.

PINK AND MAGENTA SPECKLED MOTH ORCHID

FLOWERS Outer petals with paler pink edges, shaded and speckled with a dark magenta. Inner petals of a more orangey pink.

LEAVES & STEMS Long, jointed stems with smaller branches at the top bearing 10 to 12 individual flowers.

SIZE & IMPACT These are particularly tall orchids, with many blooms on a long, arching flower head.

PERFECT FOR ... Impressive displays in large containers. Combine with strongly shaped foliage and filler plants.

VARIEGATED PINK PEONY

FLOWERS Blousy, cup-shaped blooms with large, round outer petals and smaller, feathery inner petals in mottled shades of pink.

LEAVES & STEMS Slender but sturdy stems. Pale green, lobed leaves borne near the flowers.

SIZE & IMPACT One or two flowers to each stem, between 2½ in (6.5 cm) and 4 in (10 cm) wide.

PERFECT FOR … Mixed arrangements, combined with smaller flowers in darker and paler pinks and purples.

BRIGHT PINK MOTH ORCHID

FLOWERS Outer petals in a bright, almost shocking, pink, veined in a darker shade and fading to white at the center. Clustered around small, darker inner petals.

LEAVES & STEMS Strong, slim stems with flower heads made up of open flowers and a few buds.

SIZE & IMPACT Longish flower head makes this a taller bloom with about five open flowers.

PERFECT FOR … Adding a bit of dramatic color to a mixed arrangement or combined with other colored orchids.

PINK AND PALE YELLOW PEONY

FLOWERS Large, cup-shaped flowers with petals in different shades of pink that fade to a pale, slightly orange-yellow.

LEAVES & STEMS Slim, upright stems with a handful of pale green, spear-like leaves at the top.

SIZE & IMPACT The large, colorful flowers are each about 5 in (12.5 cm) across.

PERFECT FOR … An arrangement that combines orange, yellow, and pink blooms.

PINK AND YELLOW ENGLISH ROSE

FLOWERS A loose, open style of rose with petals that are pale yellow, some streaked with pink in varying degrees. Frothy yellow stamens cluster at the center.

LEAVES & STEMS Fine, thornless stems with a few pale green leaves close to the flowers.

SIZE & IMPACT Medium to large flowers, about 4 in (10 cm) wide.

PERFECT FOR ... Combining with more delicate flowers in a wide range of different colors.

PINK POPPY

FLOWERS Large flowers with petals that have a slightly papery texture set around a distinctive darker center. The pink petals fade to a pale orange at the base.

LEAVES & STEMS Soft, slightly drooping stems with a fine downy coating, bearing a few crinkled leaves.

SIZE & IMPACT Wide flowers of about 4 in (10 cm) across with a delicate appearance.

PERFECT FOR ... Combine with other flowers or foliage that offer a contrast in texture, such as tulips and spikey grasses.

PINK PEONY BUDS

FLOWERS Globe-shaped flower buds made up of overlapping circular petals. Each petal is graduated in color from pink to white at the base.

LEAVES & STEMS Slender, branching stems that bear deeply lobed, dark green leaves.

SIZE & IMPACT Buds about 1 in (2.5 cm) in diameter are held on the end of separate stems.

PERFECT FOR ... Combining with more open, wider flowers, such as other peonies or roses.

MAGENTA CLEOME

FLOWERS Flower heads are made up of smaller individual flowers that bear a few narrow magenta petals and long, spidery stamens.

LEAVES & STEMS Thick, upright stems with leaves clustered along the stems below the blooms.

SIZE & IMPACT Large, feathery flower heads about 6 in (15 cm) in length.

PERFECT FOR ... Mixing with exotic blooms that have distinctive shapes to break up the strong lines and add texture.

VARIEGATED PINK SWEET PEA

FLOWERS A cluster of typical sweet-pea flowers with petals that are graduated from pink to white and pale lemon at the base. The petals are edged and mottled with a darker pink.

LEAVES & STEMS Thin, erect stems with a few oval leaves at the base and the occasional tendril.

SIZE & IMPACT Shortish flower head with five to six flowers

PERFECT FOR ... Adding just a hint of a stronger pink in an arrangement without it being too overpowering or using a larger flower.

PALE PINK OLD ROSE

FLOWERS An open, many-petaled rose in a pale blush pink, tinged with a darker shade. The smaller petals at the center fall open to reveal golden-yellow stamens.

LEAVES & STEMS Strong, thorned stems bearing glossy, green, slightly serrated leaves, set in groups of three.

SIZE & IMPACT Single flowers, up to 5 in (12.5 cm) across.

PERFECT FOR ... Combining with other roses in a variety of shades for an old-fashioned arrangement, or mixed with other pink blooms.

PINK HYDRANGEA

FLOWERS Large flower heads made up of many smaller individual flowers, mostly pale pink fading to white at the center, but some pale lime green.

LEAVES & STEMS Short, thick, upright stems with a few large, heart-shaped and serrated leaves.

SIZE & IMPACT Wide, rounded flower heads, 6–8 in (15–20 cm) across.

PERFECT FOR ... Mixing arrangements that combine strongly shaped and architectural flowers to create large, impressive displays.

WHITE AND PINK STRIPED TULIP

FLOWERS An open style of tulip flower, with inward curving, upright petals in white, streaked with a strong, dark pink. A prominent green ovary and yellow stamens at the center.

LEAVES & STEMS Slim, upright stems. Long, glossy leaves are borne around the base of the stem.

SIZE & IMPACT Flowers about 2 in (5 cm) long and wide, borne singly at the end of stems.

PERFECT FOR ... Combining with pink and white flowers in a mixed display.

PALE PINK TEA ROSE

FLOWERS A very delicately colored rose, with petals in the palest pink possible, fading to a near cream. The petals are tightly packed.

LEAVES & STEMS Strong, erect, thorned stems with glossy green, oval leaves with serrated edges.

SIZE & IMPACT A single, medium-sized rose that's up to 2 in (5 cm) wide.

PERFECT FOR ... Mixing with other delicate colors, or for introducing a lighter shade in a predominantly pink display.

PALE PINK TULIP

FLOWERS A goblet-shaped flower made up of few oval petals, each white at the base and along the center, with pink shading toward the edges.

LEAVES & STEMS Thick, strong stems with two long and wide leaves set at the base.

SIZE & IMPACT Single flowers, about 2 in (5 cm) long, borne singly on each stem.

PERFECT FOR ... Simple arrangements, combined with other tulips or with more delicate, smaller blooms.

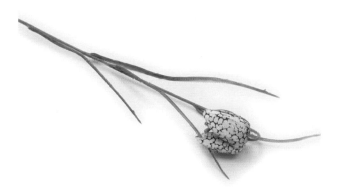

PINK MOTTLED FRITILLARY

FLOWERS A pendulous, bell-shaped flower, made up of only a few petals, each white to pale pink and mottled with a darker pink checkerboard pattern.

LEAVES & STEMS Very fine, slightly lax stems with thin, grass-like light green leaves.

SIZE & IMPACT Smallish flowers, about 1½ in (4 cm) long.

PERFECT FOR ... Combining with a few other small, spring-like flowers and light green foliage to make the most of the unusual flower heads.

WHITE AND PINK CASABLANCA LILY

FLOWERS Large flowers with arching, pointed, narow petals, shaded and mottled with pink, and with streaks of lime green leading to the center.

LEAVES & STEMS Strong, erect stems with plenty of long, spear-like, dark green leaves.

SIZE & IMPACT Exotic, large blooms, 4–6 in (10–15 cm) long, several to each stem.

PERFECT FOR ... Mixing with other large and impressive flowers, or when used as the sole flower type in an arrangement.

PINKISH MAUVE DELPHINIUM

FLOWERS Large flower spikes made up of smaller double flowers with papery petals of pinkish mauve and white.
LEAVES & STEMS Flower spikes are borne on tall, upright stems. Small branches bear feathery, light green leaves below the flowers.
SIZE & IMPACT Well-covered flower heads, about 12 in (30 cm) long.
PERFECT FOR... Adding height and substance to a display but in a delicate color.

MAUVE LOVE-IN-A-MIST

FLOWERS Delicate flowers made up of thin, pointed, mauve petals, set around a cluster of feathery green stamens.
LEAVES & STEMS Stems bear several thin, bending branches. Very fine, feathery leaves are found at the end of some stems, set below the flowers, and clustered around the axils on the stem.
SIZE & IMPACT There are several flowers to each stem, measuring up to 2 in (5 cm) across.
PERFECT FOR ... Adding a light, frothy touch to a display.

PINKISH PURPLE TULIP

FLOWERS Upright, oval flowers made up of few overlapping petals that are shaded a pinkish purple at the edges, fading to white at the center and base.
LEAVES & STEMS Long, spear-like leaves are borne at the base of a thick, fleshy stem.
SIZE & IMPACT Each medium-length stem bears one flower, about 2 in (5 cm) long.
PERFECT FOR ... Brightly colored displays – the white in the petals helps neutralize stronger shades.

MAUVE PINCUSHION

FLOWERS A frothy flower with lots of small, lobed petals in mauve, pink, and white, clustered around a center that is said to resemble a pincushion.

LEAVES & STEMS Thin, slightly lax stems. Narrow, pointed, and deeply serrated leaves borne lower down on the stems.

SIZE & IMPACT Each stem bears two to three branches with flowers in varying stages of opening.

PERFECT FOR ... Combining with more showy blooms such as roses and lilies.

MAUVE TEA ROSE

FLOWERS A traditional tea rose shape, with large mauve petals that have slightly frilled edges and whirl out from the tightly packed center.

LEAVES & STEMS Slender but strong, thornless stems, with a few leaves around the flower.

SIZE & IMPACT Small to medium, slightly open flowers, 2–3 in, (5–7.5 cm) wide.

PERFECT FOR ... Mixing with other colored tea roses to create a romantic-themed arrangement.

PURPLE LILAC

FLOWERS Long flower heads made up of a multitude of smaller, four-petaled flowers, with petals graduating from purple through to white at the center.

LEAVES & STEMS Strong, woody stems bear several heart-shaped green leaves.

SIZE & IMPACT Flower heads up to 6 in (15 cm) long and 3 in (7.5 cm) wide.

PERFECT FOR ... Using to add both height and texture in a display using purple shades.

MAUVE ALLIUM

FLOWERS A spherical flower head made up of many small, star-shaped flowers with small mauve petals set around spikey green stamens.

LEAVES & STEMS Strong, upright stems. Long, narrow, strap-like leaves at the stem's base or available separately.

SIZE & IMPACT Each flower head is borne singly on the stem and has a diameter of about 4 in (6 cm).

PERFECT FOR ... A minimal display, featuring a single species.

PURPLE AND GREEN TULIP

FLOWERS Inward-curving and slightly crinkled, the petals of this tulip are an intense purple at the margins, fading to a light, lime green at the base.

LEAVES & STEMS Fleshy, thick stems, with the two long, pointed leaves wrapped around the base.

SIZE & IMPACT Oval-shaped, typical tulip flowers, up to 3 in (7.5 cm) long.

PERFECT FOR ... Combining these strongly shaped blooms with smaller, finer flowers for a contrast in textures.

PURPLE FLOWERING MEADOW GRASS

FLOWERS A range of small, open, and sparsely petaled flowers in deep shades of purple, combined with long, delicate seed heads.

LEAVES & STEMS A mass of very thin and sharply edged bright green leaves mingled with flowering stems.

SIZE & IMPACT The clump of leaves is thick—about 3 in (7.5 cm) at the widest and about 12 in (30 cm) tall.

PERFECT FOR ... Adding a strong vertical element and a block of green color.

PURPLE MOTH ORCHID

FLOWERS Typical moth orchid flowers with both outer and inner petals in an intense, imperial purple. A few pale green buds are included on the flower head.

LEAVES & STEMS Thin, upright stems. Available with or without the wide, fleshy leaves and aerial roots.

SIZE & IMPACT Each flower head bears 10 to 12 individual blooms and five to six buds.

PERFECT FOR ... Use in a display of a single flower type, combined with a simple but impressive container.

ELDERBERRY

FLOWERS The flower clusters on these stems are at the stage where the petals have fallen and the first purple fruits are beginning to form.

LEAVES & STEMS Spear-like and deeply veined leaves with serrated edges are borne on slim, woody stems.

SIZE & IMPACT The branching stems bear several clusters, each 1½–5 in (4–12.5 cm) across.

PERFECT FOR ... When you want to add a strong color like purple but in small, delicate amounts.

VIOLETS

FLOWERS Small flowers but in a vivid shade of violet; five slightly pointed petals are clustered around a bright yellow center.

LEAVES & STEMS Soft and thin stems with small, heart-shaped green leaves.

SIZE & IMPACT Small flowers, no more than 1 in (2.5 cm) wide.

PERFECT FOR ... Use in a mass to make the most of the intense color. Combine with other small flowers to make hand-tied bouquets.

PURPLE ALLIUM

FLOWERS A mass of tiny star-like flowers in a purple shade are held in a neat, spherical shape.

LEAVES & STEMS Firm, upright stems. Available with several strap-like leaves at the base.

SIZE & IMPACT Each stem bears just one flower head with a diameter of about 4 in (6 cm).

PERFECT FOR ... Using on their own or combining with other alliums in mauve or violet. Ideal for arrangements with strong architectural shapes.

PURPLE TULIP

FLOWERS A dark-colored tulip with a tight, goblet-shaped flower. The deep purple of the petals fades to a lighter tint along the center.

LEAVES & STEMS Upright, fleshy stems with long, pointed leaves in pairs at the base.

SIZE & IMPACT Compact, oval-shaped flowers, up to 2 in (5 cm) long and borne singly on the stems.

PERFECT FOR ... Mixing with other tulips in white or lighter tints or to add a strong color.

PURPLE COW PARSLEY

FLOWERS Delicate flower heads made up of small, purple indvidual flowers and pale green buds, borne on thin stems in an umbrella shape.

LEAVES & STEMS Thin bending stems with a few lobed, serrated leaves.

SIZE & IMPACT Tall stems with several branches, each bearing one frothy flower head about 2 in (5 cm) wide.

PERFECT FOR ... Use to add a lighter texture when combined with larger flowers in a mixed display.

DEEP PURPLE, WILD AGAPANTHUS

FLOWERS Flower heads are made up of a large clump of fine stems, most of which bear deep purple, six-petaled, star-like flowers.

LEAVES & STEMS Thick, upright stems are topped with a mass of finer stems.

SIZE & IMPACT The large, multiple flower heads measure 8–10 in (20–25 cm) across.

PERFECT FOR … Use in an intact clump to add a large area of highly textured purple color, or break up into smaller sections and to add detail.

DARK PURPLE PANSIES

FLOWERS Large-petaled pansies in a shade that's so dark it's almost black. Stems bear flowers in various stages, from completely open to tight buds.

LEAVES & STEMS Small, round leaves, held toward the base of short, fine stems.

SIZE & IMPACT The open flowers are about 1 in (2.5 cm) across, the smaller buds no more than ¼ in (5 mm) long.

PERFECT FOR … Adding a deep shade to a display at strategic points.

PURPLE JASMINE

FLOWERS Stems bear several flower heads made up of tiny, violet-blue flowers, held on fine, smaller stems and accompanied by long tendrils.

LEAVES & STEMS Long, slim, twining stems, with many branches and small, sword-like, serrated leaves.

SIZE & IMPACT Flower heads vary in size; some have just a few individual flowers while others have 25–30 blooms.

PERFECT FOR … Adding width to a display, especially if allowed to fall forward and over the vase.

DEEP VIOLET VANDA ORCHID

FLOWERS Long flower heads made up of five-petaled individual blooms and a few small buds. The petals are a deep violet, veined in a darker shade of the same.

LEAVES & STEMS Very long, slender stems with flower heads at the top. Long, strappy leaves are available.

SIZE & IMPACT The flower head is 12–16 in (30–40 cm) long; the individual flowers are 1–2 in (2.5–5 cm) wide.

PERFECT FOR … Using as statement flowers (used singly or in small groups) because of their large size.

LAVENDER

FLOWERS Spikey flower heads made up of tiny flowers, more open at the tip than at the base. Each lavender clump bears several spikes.

LEAVES & STEMS Short, spikey leaves cover the stems. Each clump bears many flowering and non-flowering stems.

SIZE & IMPACT Flower heads are about 1½ in (4 cm) long; each clump has 12–15 flower heads.

PERFECT FOR … Adding textural interest with the small pointed leaves and short flower spikes.

LARGE VIOLET ALLIUM

FLOWERS The largest of the alliums, with big, spherical flower heads made up of a multitude of tiny, star-shaped flowers, clustered round green centers.

LEAVES & STEMS Very long, thick, and fleshy stems with flowers borne singly. Available with foliage attached.

SIZE & IMPACT Large, globe-shaped flower heads, up to 9 in (23 cm) wide.

PERFECT FOR … Truly grand displays because of these blooms.

VIOLET AND PINK SWEET PEA

FLOWERS Typical sweet-pea flowers, with the larger petals colored with different shades of violet, purple, and pink, and the much smaller petals in red.

LEAVES & STEMS Thin, upright stems, with some oval leaves borne toward the base and a few tendrils.

SIZE & IMPACT Flower heads about 7 in (18 cm) long and made up of five to six blooms.

PERFECT FOR ... Adding a twist of bold color to a more traditional arrangement.

BLUE AGAPANTHUS

FLOWERS Many light blue, trumpet-shaped individual flowers are held on fine stems to make up large umbrella-shaped flower heads.

LEAVES & STEMS Glossy, strap-like leaves are held at the base of strong, thick stems, or available separately.

SIZE & IMPACT There is one multiple flower head to each stem, measuring about 6 in (15 cm) across.

PERFECT FOR ... When you want a strong blue that will stand out in an arrangement.

BLUE DELPHINIUM

FLOWERS Fluffy, open individual flowers are borne in long spikes that include a few buds. Pale blue, papery-textured petals surround a small white center.

LEAVES & STEMS Tall, upright stems bear the flower spikes at the end. Feathery leaves are held just below the flowers.

SIZE & IMPACT The thick flower heads are covered with blooms. Spikes up to 12 in (30 cm) long.

PERFECT FOR ... Adding height and bulking out the background in a mixed display.

BLUE WILD CLEMATIS

FLOWERS Each stem bears several clumps of tiny blue flowers with wispy, yellow stamens.

LEAVES & STEMS Long, slim stems with plenty of glossy, green, spear-like leaves and a few twining tendrils.

SIZE & IMPACT Individual flowers are small, about ½ in (1 cm) wide, but borne in small clumps.

PERFECT FOR … If you want a tall plant that's not too solid in its shape; the small blue flowers and pointed leaves can break up the background of an arrangement.

BLUE HYDRANGEA

FLOWERS A small, rounded flower head made up of a cluster of simple, four-petaled flowers in faded blue or tinged with green.

LEAVES & STEMS Heart-shaped leaves with slightly serrated edges form a collar under the flower head.

SIZE & IMPACT Flower heads are about 4 in (10 cm) across but the leaves extend the width to about 5½ in (14 cm).

PERFECT FOR … Adding small clusters of an interesting shade of blue.

PALE GREEN HYDRANGEA

FLOWERS A larger flower head with many light green, individual, four-petaled flowers. The edges of some petals are tinged with a contrasting red.

LEAVES & STEMS Thick, sturdy stems and heart-shaped leaves, held close to the flower heads.

SIZE & IMPACT Wide, domed flower heads, up to 8 in (20 cm) across.

PERFECT FOR … Making a strong focal point because of the distinctive color of these flowers.

MULTICOLORED MOTH ORCHID

FLOWERS Outer petals are a pale, lime green, mottled with a maroon shade. The small inner petals are a vivid magenta.

LEAVES & STEMS Strong, upright stems and thick fleshy leaves, which can be obtained separately.

SIZE & IMPACT Six to eight flowers about 2 in (5 cm) wide and a few buds in varying sizes.

PERFECT FOR … Combining with other colored orchids – particularly magenta – to create an exotic-looking arrangement.

PALE GREEN VIBURNUM

FLOWERS Dense flower heads made up of a mass of delicate, small, pale green flowers.

LEAVES & STEMS Long twiggy stems that branch at the top into smaller green stems bearing the flowers. Large lobed leaves are borne on the smaller flowering stems.

SIZE & IMPACT Stems bear two to three flower heads varying in size from 2–5 in (5–12.5 cm)

PERFECT FOR … Combine with large single blooms, such as roses and peonies.

LAMBS' EARS SPRAY

FLOWERS Flowerless.

LEAVES & STEMS Oval-shaped leaves, slightly wider near the top and tapering to a point. Some tinged with red. All mottled on the right side with a faint silvery bloom. The spray of leaves is made up of several fine twiggy stems.

SIZE & IMPACT Leaves are about 2 in (5 cm) long. Sprays are about 16 in (40 cm) long and up to 12 in (30 cm) across.

PERFECT FOR … If you want a background foliage that has more visual interest than plain green.

THISTLE SEED PODS

FLOWERS Several green seed pods, shaped like large rose hips. Each seed head is lightly covered with small red bristles; a cluster of red bristles can be seen just inside each one.
LEAVES & STEMS Each stem bears two to three branches, bearing two seed pods. The heart-shaped leaves are grey green, with light green fronds emerging from the leaf axils.
SIZE & IMPACT Seed heads vary from 1–1½ in (2.5–4 cm) in length. They are held on long, slightly twisting stems.
PERFECT FOR … Strongly architectural displays.

SKIMMIA

FLOWERS A few clusters of tiny greenish-brown flowers held at the end of separate branches.
LEAVES & STEMS Tall, upright stems with upright branches bearing several large oval leaves. The grey-green foliage has a light downy coating.
SIZE & IMPACT The flower heads are up to 2 in (5 cm) across and the leaves are 2–3 in (5–7.5 cm) long.
PERFECT FOR … Adding a variety of green shades and a combination of textures.

ALLIUM BUDS

FLOWERS The slender buds of large alliums; bulbous at the base, each bud tapers off to a long, fine tip. Buds are green but slightly marked with a darker brown-green.
LEAVES & STEMS Very long, very slender leafless stems that droop slightly with the weight of the buds.
SIZE & IMPACT Each stem bears just one bud, measuring about 8 in (20 cm) long.
PERFECT FOR … Adding a long, flowing, linear element to an arrangement.

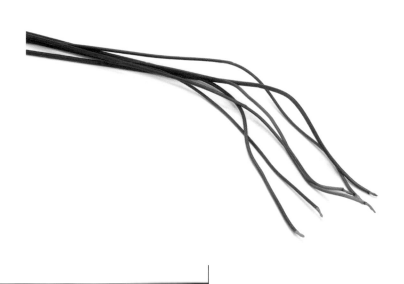

ONION GRASS

FLOWERS Flowerless.

LEAVES & STEMS Very long, tubular, grass-like leaves – somewhat similar to the leaves of chives – that are not attached to a stem.

SIZE & IMPACT Each separate onion grass is around 3 ft (1 m) long, but only about ¼ in (5 mm) wide.

PERFECT FOR ... Adding a graphic element to an arrangement – the lines will be slightly curving and will lean rather than be vertical.

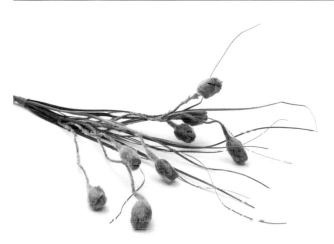

BUNNY TAIL GRASS

FLOWERS Several egg-shaped seed heads, each with a cross-shaped slit in the top, borne on slightly twisting stems. Both seed heads and stems have a downy coating.

LEAVES & STEMS A small clump of grass-like leaves, from which the seed head stems emerge.

SIZE & IMPACT The seed heads are about 1½ in (4 cm) long and are held on the ends of individual stems.

PERFECT FOR ... Adding an unusual element to a display or creating a contrast of textures.

THYME

FLOWERS Insignificant flowers are borne among the leaves.

LEAVES & STEMS Thin, twiggy stems that divide into several fine branches. The tiny leaves are borne in small clumps, spaced along the length of each branch.

SIZE & IMPACT The leaves are very small, no more than ¼ in (5 mm) long, held in clumps of five with the minute flowers in between.

PERFECT FOR ... Combining thyme stems with soft-petaled flowers to add a spikey green visual accent.

MEADOW GRASS

FLOWERS Flowerless.
LEAVES & STEMS Very long and thin leaves, with a slight crease along the center, tapering to a sharp point. The blades are held in groups of 12 to 15 on short stems.
SIZE & IMPACT Each blade is about ¼ in (5 mm) wide, tapering to a point, and 12–15 in (30–38 cm) long.
PERFECT FOR … Use in a big bunch if you want to include strong vertical lines, or add individual blades to break up solid shapes and hard lines.

PLANTAIN LEAVES

FLOWERS Flowerless.
LEAVES & STEMS Wide, almost circular, leaves that narrow to a pointed tip. The wide stems are almost part of the leaf itself. Each leaf is markedly ribbed.
SIZE & IMPACT The leaves are fairly wide – about 4 in (10 cm) across – and about 6 in (15 cm) long. The stems are short, no more than 4 in (10 cm) long.
PERFECT FOR … Using toward the base of an arrangement because of the short-stemmed leaves.

CAMELLIA FOLIAGE

FLOWERS Flowerless.
LEAVES & STEMS Tall, stiff, slightly knobbly stems with several branches. The leaves are oval and slightly glossy and have faintly serrated edges.
SIZE & IMPACT Each branch is well covered with good-sized darkish green leaves, each about 2½ in (6.5 cm) long.
PERFECT FOR … If you need a strong background of well-shaped green leaves. Divide the stems into smaller sections and use to add a darker shade of green.

SEA HOLLY

FLOWERS Thistle-like, egg-shaped, purple-green flower heads covered with greyish bristles.

LEAVES & STEMS Upright branching stems that bear clumps of slightly prickly-looking leaves around the flowers and at the axils of the branching stems.

SIZE & IMPACT The flowers are about 1½ in (4 cm) long, held at the end of each branch.

PERFECT FOR … Mixing with purple and blue flowers to add a more subtle grey-green shade.

EUCALYPTUS FOLIAGE

FLOWERS Flowerless.

LEAVES & STEMS Blue-green, round leaves with very slight points are borne in pairs along thin, twiggy stems.

SIZE & IMPACT The leaves vary in size from about ¾ in (2 cm) to 2 in (5 cm) wide, with the smallest set at the top of each stem and graduating in size to the largest at the base.

PERFECT FOR … Playing up the blue color in an arrangement, or if you want a foliage in a shade of green that's subtle.

UMBRELLA PAPYRUS

FLOWERS Flowerless.

LEAVES & STEMS Long, upright stems that are segmented like bamboo. The grass-like leaves emerge in a bunch from the top of each stem.

SIZE & IMPACT The spreading leaf clumps measure 10–12 in (25–30 cm) across and are borne on fairly long stems.

PERFECT FOR … Use in any display where you want foliage with plenty of height that will be visible at the top of the arrangement.

WATER-LILY LEAVES

FLOWERS Flowerless.
LEAVES & STEMS Very large, virtually circular, leaves, divided at the top. Each leaf is strongly marked with a few deep veins. Thick, pale green, rope-like stems bear one leaf each.
SIZE & IMPACT The wide leaves are about 8 in (20 cm) across and are held on gently twining stems that stretch out to 18–24 in (45–60 cm) long.
PERFECT FOR ... Use when you need a large and distinctively shaped leaf.

BAMBOO LEAVES

FLOWERS Flowerless.
LEAVES & STEMS Slim but strong stems with many knobbly joints. Smaller, finer branches along the main stem bear the sword-like leaves, some tipped with a rusty brown shade.
SIZE & IMPACT The leaves are about 3 in (7.5 cm) long and are held in groups of five at the end of each branch.
PERFECT FOR ... Making an ideal background because the tall branching stems present an interesting outline when combined with large, exotic blooms.

MEADOW GRASS CLUMP

FLOWERS Flowerless.
LEAVES & STEMS Tall, stiff blades of grass that vary in shade from light to medium green. Each blade is creased along the center and tapers to a long, fine point at the tip.
SIZE & IMPACT Numerous blades of grass are bound together, close to the base, to form a tight clump about 3 in (7.5 cm) wide (at the base) and about 28 in (70 cm) long.
PERFECT FOR ... When you need a dense area of solid green in a display.

BUDDING TWIGS

FLOWERS Flowerless.

LEAVES & STEMS Several thin, woody twigs – brown at the bottom and green at the top – that are joined together by smaller branches to form a latticework. A few small, oval leaves are dotted along the green sections of the stems.

SIZE & IMPACT The twigs can be stretched out into quite a long lattice, or drawn up into a bundle.

PERFECT FOR ... Forming an interesting background and adding a support for flowers with soft, drooping stems.

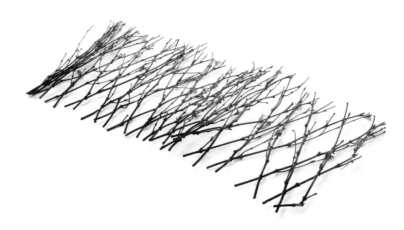

BELLS OF IRELAND

FLOWERS A long flower spike made up of numerous green blooms: the green "petals" are calyxes; the white true flowers are held at the center of the calyxes.

LEAVES & STEMS Tall, pliable, leafless stems, with the flower heads taking up most of the length.

SIZE & IMPACT Each flower head is 12–14 in (30–35 cm) long, with individual blooms no more than 1½ in (4 cm) wide.

PERFECT FOR ... Use as an alternative to green foliage; ideal when combined with other white and green blooms.

CACTUS FLOWER

FLOWERS Distinctive, egg-shaped flower heads in a pale lime green, with each segment tipped with brown.

LEAVES & STEMS Stiff, upright stems that are clothed with narrow, grey-green leaves that have sharply serrated edges.

SIZE & IMPACT The flower head is about 2 in (5 cm) long, with a clump of leaves about 1½ in (4 cm) emerging at the top.

PERFECT FOR ... Combining with other exotics to add height and interesting texture.

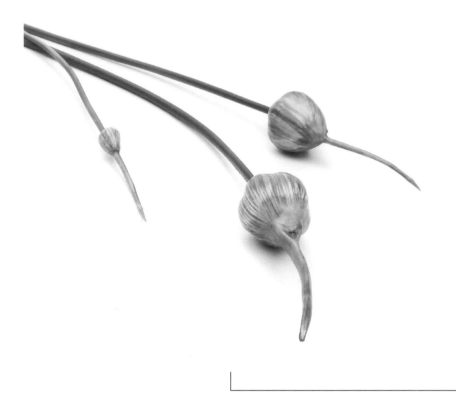

ONION BUDS

FLOWERS The unopened buds of onion flowers, bulbous at the base and then with elongated green tips. The bases are yellow streaked with purple.

LEAVES & STEMS Individual buds are held on long, lax, leafless stems that droop with the weight of the buds.

SIZE & IMPACT The stems – about 28 in (70 cm) long – bear single buds, 1½–3 in (4–7.5 cm) long.

PERFECT FOR … Adding long, arching lines that fan out from a display.

LADY'S MANTLE

FLOWERS Frothy clusters made up very tiny, star-like, lime-green flowers and held on thin, branching stems.

LEAVES & STEMS Long, thin, upright main stems with several spreading branches bearing the flower heads. Slightly lobed, fan-shaped leaves.

SIZE & IMPACT Stems bear eight to ten flower heads, 2–3 in (5–7.5 cm) across.

PERFECT FOR … Adding a delicate, light green shade to a mixed arrangement.

BIRCH TWIGS

FLOWERS Flowerless.

LEAVES & STEMS Thin, stiff stems with several branches fanning out from the same point that divide into fine twigs. The bright, yellow-green leaves are held on thin, white, sinuous twigs.

SIZE & IMPACT Although tiny – less than ½ in (1 cm) long – the leaves are brightly colored.

PERFECT FOR … Combining with large blooms, such as peonies and roses, to break up the outline of a display.

MEADOW CAT'S TAIL

FLOWERS Long flower heads made up of a multitude of
miniscule, spherical flowers and fine, fluffy down.
LEAVES & STEMS The flower heads are borne on fine
branches that emerge from grass-like leaves held on a
short stem. The leaves have red edges and a darker
green central rib.
SIZE & IMPACT The soft, pliable flower heads are up to
5 in (12.5 cm) long, about the same length as the leaves.
PERFECT FOR ... Arrangements that combine flowers and
foliage in a variety of shades of green.

PLUMOSA FERN

FLOWERS Flowerless.
LEAVES & STEMS Fine twiggy stems with one leaf at the
top and then others alternating along the stem. Each leaf
pointed with saw-tooth-like serrations along the edges.
SIZE & IMPACT Long stems with several leaves along the top
section and then with shorter, leaf-bearing branches lower
down. The leaves are 1½–3 in (4–7.5 cm) long.
PERFECT FOR ... The spreading habit of the leaves and the
upright stems make this ideal for background foliage.

GREEN TACA ORCHID

FLOWERS Composite blooms with a group
of lime-green, six-petaled flowers and green-
and-red buds at the center of three pale
lemon petals that are veined with burgundy.
Wispy, pale yellow fronds hang down from
the center.
LEAVES & STEMS Slim but strong upright
stems bearing a single bloom.
SIZE & IMPACT The flowers are
6–8 in (15–20 cm) long.
PERFECT FOR ... If you want a striking and
unusual flower that will be the focal point of
the display.

DILL

FLOWERS Masses of tiny, yellow-green, individual flowers form flat, umbrella-shaped flower heads.
LEAVES & STEMS Pliable, upright stems with a faint, downy coating. Just a few feathery leaves are found on each stem.
SIZE & IMPACT Each stem bears one flower head about 6 in (15 cm) wide.
PERFECT FOR ... Creating a delicate outline to a display or adding an interesting green shade.

BUTTERCUPS

FLOWERS Small, golden-yellow, five-petaled flowers, combined with smaller, spikey, round, green seed heads.
LEAVES & STEMS Each main stem bears many finer branching stems, with the flowers at the ends. A few deeply lobed leaves are found toward the base.
SIZE & IMPACT Although the flowers and seed heads are small, each stem provides a spray of color and interest.
PERFECT FOR ... Adding small points of golden-yellow in a mixed arrangement.

YELLOW FREESIA

FLOWERS Flower heads made up of bright yellow, funnel-shaped individual flowers. The blooms at the top of each stem are unfurled; those at the base are fully open.
LEAVES & STEMS Fine, flexible stems with two or three flower-bearing branches and two sword-like leaves.
SIZE & IMPACT The densely covered flower heads are 2–5 in (5–12.5 cm) long.
PERFECT FOR ... Combining with purple blooms when you want to create a display of contrasting colors.

LADY SLIPPER ORCHID

FLOWERS Pale lemon, ruffled petals, marked with dark red-brown lines, stand above and below the central red-green pouch. Elongated and similarly marked yellow petals emerge from either side of the pouch.

LEAVES & STEMS Long, stiff stems, carrying a single flower.

SIZE & IMPACT The flowers are 10–12 in (25–30 cm) long, with the elongated petals measuring up to 35 in (90 cm) long.

PERFECT FOR … Combining with other lady slipper orchids and with distinctive foliage.

TWISTED PUSSY WILLOW

FLOWERS Fluffy, open, yellow-green catkins borne in small clusters on rusty brown twigs.

LEAVES & STEMS Twisting, woody twigs, dusted with a mossy-green lichen. The sprays bear just a few lobed leaves.

SIZE & IMPACT Large, branching sprays of twigs. The catkins are no more than 3/8 in (1 cm) wide and are held in clusters of six.

PERFECT FOR … Use as a filler plant to add a twisting, graphic line to a display.

WILD HONEYSUCKLE

FLOWERS Yellow and cream, trumpet-shaped flowers in small clusters.

LEAVES & STEMS Oval leaves are held in pairs along thin, tapering stems with the smallest at the very top. The flower clusters are found toward the middle of some stems.

SIZE & IMPACT Smallish flowers – about 1 in (2.5 cm) long – and leaves on the long stems.

PERFECT FOR … Using stems individually or in groups to add height in mixed arrangements.

BRONZE FENNEL

FLOWERS Umbrella-shaped flower heads composed of tiny, bronzed, budding flowers.
LEAVES & STEMS Slim, erect stems with a few nodules along the length and feathery bronze leaves near the base.
SIZE & IMPACT Although the individual flower buds are tiny, they combine to make a cluster about 5 in (12.5 cm) wide.
PERFECT FOR ... With flower heads in a subtle and interesting color, these tall, delicate blooms work well with large-petaled flowers in dusky shades.

MAGNOLIA

FLOWERS Pure white, goblet-shaped flowers made up of oval petals set around a green and yellow starry center, and down-covered, egg-shaped flower buds.
LEAVES & STEMS Knobbly, branching, woody stems bearing flowers, buds, and a few large oval leaves.
SIZE & IMPACT Distinctive flowers, up to 4 in (10 cm) long, with smaller buds no more than 1 in (2.5 cm) long.
PERFECT FOR ... Displays that feature other white blooms or other spring-flowering plants.

PUSSY WILLOW

FLOWERS Small, silvery-grey catkins with a soft, fluffy texture, each one a slightly bent oval shape.
LEAVES & STEMS The catkins alternate along the twiggy stems, interspersed with few leaves.
SIZE & IMPACT The small catkins – no more than ½ in (1 cm) long – are found along the entire length of the stem.
PERFECT FOR ... Using with flowers and foliage that have a spreading habit because the upright stems have no branches and their linear form makes a good contrast with these flowers.

WHITE GYPSOPHILA

FLOWERS Long, drooping clusters of small, white, five-petaled flowers.

LEAVES & STEMS Thin, leafless stems branch into three or four thinner stems that in turn divide into many very fine green stems that bear the flowers.

SIZE & IMPACT The small flowers – no more than ¼ in (5 mm) wide – form clusters about 6 in (15 cm) long.

PERFECT FOR … Adding to a display so the long flower heads can droop outward.

QUEEN ANNE'S LACE

FLOWERS Delicate, frothy flower heads made up of a myriad of tiny white flowers held on spidery stems.

LEAVES & STEMS Thin, upright stems with several branches that are topped by the flower heads. A few feathery leaves.

SIZE & IMPACT The flat, umbrella-shaped flower heads are 2–3 in (5–7.5 cm) across.

PERFECT FOR … Combining with lots of different flowers – such as cottage-garden favorites like delphiniums, roses, and hydrangeas – to create an impressive mixed display.

WHITE AMARYLLIS

FLOWERS Large, soft-petaled, exotic flowers. The white, pointed petals are graduated with pale yellow and green at the base.

LEAVES & STEMS Very thick, fleshy, upright stems with no leaves.

SIZE & IMPACT Each stem bears three or four indivdual blooms that form a combined flower head of around 6 in (15 cm) diameter.

PERFECT FOR … Using alone or in a large bunch. Combine with the leaves of other exotics.

WHITE VIBURNUM

FLOWERS Rounded flower heads composed of dainty, white individual flowers, each borne on a fine, green stem.
LEAVES & STEMS The main stem is brown and twiggy and branches into thinner green stems that bear the flowers. The three-lobed leaves are carried on the green stems.
SIZE & IMPACT Stems bear three to four good-sized flower heads, up to 3 in (7.5 cm) across.
PERFECT FOR … Combining with other white flowers, or mix with red or purple flowers for a strong contrast.

WHITE RANUNCULUS

FLOWERS Tightly packed, rose-like flowers that are made up of a mass of overlapping white petals with a greenish tint.
LEAVES & STEMS Thick, flexible, light green stems. The feathery, deeply lobed leaves are held near the flowers.
SIZE & IMPACT Each stem branches into two to carry two flowers, with one bloom usually larger than the other. The flowers are up to 2 in (5 cm) wide.
PERFECT FOR … Using these densely petaled flowers with more delicate, frothy blooms, such as cow parsley.

WHITE ALLIUM

FLOWERS Globe-like flower heads composed of numerous starry white flowers. Each individual flower is shaded with green at the center.
LEAVES & STEMS Thick, upright stems that are available with a clump of glossy, strap-like leaves.
SIZE & IMPACT Each stem bears one flower head that's about 4 in (10 cm) wide.
PERFECT FOR … Combining with alliums in shades of purple when you want to add light and avoid creating a monochromatic display.

WHITE PEONY

FLOWERS The outer petals of these large, cup-shaped white flowers are circular, while the inner petals are slender with feathery edges.

LEAVES & STEMS Long, upright stems with dark green, deeply lobed leaves.

SIZE & IMPACT Each stem bears two individual blooms in different sizes; the smaller is about 2½ in (6.5 cm), the large about 3 in (7.5 cm).

PERFECT FOR ... Using with other white flowers, such as roses, hydrangeas, and tulips, for a single-color display.

WHITE POPPY

FLOWERS Large, papery petals, blotched with a dark, burgundy-brown color, set around a prominent green ovary and yellow stamens.

LEAVES & STEMS Thin, pliable stems with two or three highly ruffled leaves lower down the stem.

SIZE & IMPACT Medium-sized white flowers, up to 3 in (7.5 cm) across.

PERFECT FOR ... Combining with grasses and wildflowers for an open, fresh-looking arrangement.

WHITE CALLA LILY

FLOWERS Unusual flowers, made up of a single white spathe that's wrapped around a protruding white spadix. On the outside, the spathe is tinged with green; inside it's tinged with yellow.

LEAVES & STEMS Thick, leafless stems.

SIZE & IMPACT Distinctive flowers, up to 6 in (12.5 cm) long, are borne on the top of tall stems.

PERFECT FOR ... Mixing with other exotics, such as orchids and lilies, for an opulent, luxurious look.

WHITE NARCISSUS

FLOWERS Small clusters of white flowers, with petals edged faintly in pink. Individual flowers feature central trumpets, tinged with green, and six outer petals.

LEAVES & STEMS Straight, sturdy stems with a few narrow, strap-like leaves at the base.

SIZE & IMPACT Small flowers, less than 1 in (2.5 cm) across, are held in clusters of just a few blooms.

PERFECT FOR ... Combining with white tulips and daffodils; also combine with dark green foliage for a sparkling display.

WHITE MOTH ORCHID

FLOWERS The large outer petals are a pure, brilliant white. The tiny inner petals are tinged with green and red and flecked with darker red.

LEAVES & STEMS Strong, slim stems bear flower heads of four to five blooms and several buds.

SIZE & IMPACT Individual blooms, about 1½ in (4 cm) across, form flower heads 6–8 in (15–20 cm) long.

PERFECT FOR ... Using in groups of just a few specimens for minimal but spectacular displays.

WHITE HYDRANGEA

FLOWERS Large, rounded flower heads made up of many flowers with bright white petals set around a small green center.

LEAVES & STEMS Short, thick stems with large, heart-shaped leaves just below the flower head.

SIZE & IMPACT Each stem bears one flower head about 6 in (15 cm) wide.

PERFECT FOR ... Large-scale displays, combined with showy blooms.

WHITE DAFFODIL

FLOWERS Delicate white flowers; the slim central trumpet is surrounded by six slim petals. Golden-yellow stamens are visible inside the trumpet.

LEAVES & STEMS Pliable, ribbed stems with three or four strap-like leaves wrapped around the base.

SIZE & IMPACT Small flowers, up to 2 in (5 cm) long, are borne in pairs on the top of the stems.

PERFECT FOR ... Using singly or in small groups; present in pots for a natural-looking display.

WHITE JAPANESE SPIREA

FLOWERS Loose, open flower heads composed of a cluster of many small, white, individual five-petaled flowers, each one with a tiny yellow center.

LEAVES & STEMS Tall, slender, twiggy stems. The glossy, dark green, pointed oval leaves have serrated edges.

SIZE & IMPACT Medium-sized flower heads, about 3 in (7.5 cm) across.

PERFECT FOR ... Combining with dark-colored foliage and bright, white flowers; this is ideal for adding both light and shade.

WHITE PARROT TULIP

FLOWERS Typical tulip-shaped flowers, but with petals that are delicately fringed at the edges. The white petals feature a soft pink smudge along the center.

LEAVES & STEMS Thick, pliable stems with two long, pointed leaves wrapped around the base.

SIZE & IMPACT Each stem carries one flower about 2½ in (6.5 cm) long.

PERFECT FOR ... Combining with other white flowers when you want to add a hint of color.

WHITE CASABLANCA LILY

FLOWERS Large, exotic-looking flowers with long, arching, pointed petals, speckled with rusty flecks and shaded with a creamy pink.

LEAVES & STEMS Tall, upright stems with abundant, long, spear-like bright green leaves.

SIZE & IMPACT Flowers, up to 4–6 in (10–15 cm) across, combined with unopened buds, up to 3 in (7.5 cm) long.

PERFECT FOR ... Mixing with other impressive or exotic blooms to create a dramatic display.

WHITE CYMBIDIUM ORCHID

FLOWERS An orchid with more delicate flowers; the slender white petals are flecked with small magenta spots at the base and set around a yellowish-brown center.

LEAVES & STEMS Long, segmented stems with tall, slender leaves and twiggy aerial roots held at the base.

SIZE & IMPACT Slender flower heads, up to 10 in (25 cm) long, bearing a few unopened buds at the tip.

PERFECT FOR ... Using on their own in groups of five or more, to make the most of their elegant form.

WHITE AND BLUSH OLD ROSE

FLOWERS Round, almost spherical, flowers made up of tightly packed, large white petals, each one rimmed with a delicate blush pink.

LEAVES & STEMS Thick, stiff stems with pointed oval leaves arranged in groups of five.

SIZE & IMPACT Each stem bears one or sometimes two flowers, about 4 in (10 cm) wide.

PERFECT FOR ... Combining with other old roses in different shades of pink to create a romantic, traditional-looking display.

RESOURCES

This is a selection of specialist stores that sell faux (silk) flowers,
and the equipment and additional items required to arrange them.

Silk Flowers by Sylvia
www.silkflowersbysylvia.com

Anderson Floral
www.afloral.com

Arranged for you…
www.arrangingsupplies.com

Floral Supply
www.floralsupply.com

Floral Supply Online
www.floralsupplyonline.com

Floral Supply Syndicate
www.fss.com

Flowers by Design
www.flowers-by-design.com

Gifts and Florals
www.giftsandflorals.com

Marshall Floral Products
www.marshallfloralproducts.com

Michaels
www.michaels.com

Save on Crafts
www.save-on-crafts.com

Further Reading

Color: How to Use Color in Art and Design
Edith Anderson Feisner, 2006, Laurence King

The Complete Guide to Flower Arranging
Jane Packer, new edition 1998, Dorling Kindersley

INDEX

ACKNOWLEDGMENTS

This book would not have been possible without the wonderful Caroline Smith, who helped me to write it and style the photography. The photographs for *Beautifully Bold Faux Flowers* were taken by the talented Elizabeth Zeschin and the equally capable Simon Pask. It was a pleasure to see designer Dave Jones create the finished pages with such elegance.

Thanks also go to the team at Quantum: Publisher Sarah Bloxham for her drive and vision, Managing Editor Samantha Warrington for ensuring everything happened as it should, and Assistant Editor Jo Morley for supporting every stage of the process. Finally, Rohana Yosuf for ensuring the book you hold in your hands was printed to the highest possible standard.

Closer to home, Jenny Freeman has always been ready to help out, and Mel Crossman for many years has given me her cheerful, practical assistance. Particular thanks go to my son, Jonathan, who sourced many of my flowers throughout Asia and Europe. Lastly but by no means least, I thank my husband, Michael, who enthusiastically backed my publishing this book and has been my mainstay throughout my career in floral design.